THE STIRRING WORLD OF ROBERT CAREY

Robert Carey's Memoirs 1577 – 1625

The Stirring World of Robert Carey

by

Robert Carey

Robert Carey's Memoirs were first published in 1759 by the Earl of Corke and Orrery.

Reprinted in 1808 by Constable, with additional passages by Sir Walter Scott.

A third edition was edited by GH Powell in 1905 and published by Alexander Moring Limited, London.

ISBN 1-904466-29-X

Website: www.RippingYarns.com

Cover Illustrations

Photographs, © The Borderers 2004.
Photographs in the appendix and the cover photographs, reproduced by kind permission of The Borderers.

Printed by
Lightning Source.

THE STIRRING WORLD OF ROBERT CAREY

CONTENTS

Editor's Introduction   7

PREFACE

The Author of the Memoirs	11
Carey's Birth and Death	12
His Early Career	12
His Marriage	13
His Wardenship of the Marches	14
Carey and the Queen	14
Accession of James I	16
Expedition to Spain	17
Editions of the Memoirs	17

THE MEMOIRS

Early Days	21
The Spanish Armada	26
In France with Lord Essex	28
First Actions on the Scottish Border	36
Marriage and the Queen's Disapproval	39
Wardenship of the East March	45
Wardenship of the Middle March	55
The Death of Queen Elizabeth and the Ride to Edinburgh	63
In the Court of King James	69

APPENDICES

1	Robert Carey's Letters	83
2	Links	87
3	Other Suggested Reading	88
4	Other Books from Ripping Yarns.com	89
5	Pictures from "The Borderers"	91

About Ripping Yarns.com   95

Editor's Introduction

Immortalised in the history books for his ride from London to Edinburgh on the death of Elizabeth I, there was much more to Robert Carey than that. He was the most successful of the "March Wardens" – a dangerous and violent occupation.

In the 1590's the English-Scottish borderlands were a violent and turbulent place. Thieves (the so-called Border reivers) would steal over from Scotland and plunder the English countryside, by force of arms if necessary.

Robert Carey had to stop them.

His memoirs give an insight into what life was really like in those troubled times. They also gave a rare glimpse into the personality and temper of Queen Elizabeth I – where losing her favour could be synonymous with losing one's head.

I shall leave it up to the reader to discover if Carey was more troubled by the Queen, the reivers or the Spanish Armada...

Ian H. Robertson, Findon, Aberdeenshire 2005

Preface

The preface is from the 1905 edition, by GH Powell.

The Author of the Memoirs

The Memoirs here presented to the reader may be said to combine every interest which can attach to this class of literature.

Brief, authentic, readable and crammed with human and contemporary interest, they form perhaps the most vivid personal record we possess of the most picturesque and romantic age in English History. As to that it might be sufficient to say that the author, Robert Carey, was a popular and spirited young nobleman, a contemporary of Shakespeare, a near relative and intimate acquaintance of Queen Elizabeth, and an eye-witness of the repulse of the Spanish Armada. In addition to these guarantees for the historical interest of his biography, he also enjoyed exceptional opportunities for observing the actual condition of the Scottish Borders at the close of the sixteenth century: a fact which sufficiently explains the great interest taken in his memoirs by their anonymous editor of 1808, who subsequently proved to be none other than Sir Walter Scott himself – the "Wizard" whose wand was to revive for modern readers the age to which these records belong and the scene of their author's greatest activity.

To anticipate Carey's lively descriptions of the "stirring world" in which he lived, or even to sketch more than the bare outline of his life, would be merely to impair the reader's pleasure in the perusal of so genuine and living a historical document.

It is doubtless to be regretted that we know little more of the writer than he himself records in a biography which does not tell us directly even the date of his birth, and only the day of the week, not the month or year, of some of the most important events of his time.

When we consider, however, the numerous adventures and intrigues in which the writer was incessantly occupied we may wonder that one, to whom the sword came so much handier than the pen, found leisure to think of posterity at all.

Carey's Birth and Death

Robert Carey, Baron Leppington and first Earl of Monmouth, was born in 1560 – the exact date is not disclosed in the memoirs – and died in 1639. He was the tenth son of Sir Henry Carey, Lord Hunsdon (1559), who is briefly described by a contemporaneous biographer as an honest stout-hearted man, who, if something of a braggart and a "ruffler," nevertheless possessed the confidence of his friends and his sovereign, and held the office of Lord Chamberlain, subsequently enjoyed by his son.

His Early Career

Young Carey received a liberal education according to the ideas of the time, under "tutors and governors," and commenced his official life at the age of seventeen when he spent a winter on the Continent as a member of the suite of Sir Thomas Layton, who was at first the Queen's Ambassador to the "United Netherlands" at Brussels, and subsequently to Don John of Austria at Luxemburg.

Four years later we find Robert Carey among the select company appointed by Queen Elizabeth to do honour to her suitor the Duc d'Alençon (better known as Duc d'Anjou) during the latter's stay in England and afterwards upon his return to the Continent.

He accompanied Secretary Walsingham to Scotland in 1583, was himself employed on several very confidential missions to James VI, and in 1587 took part with the Earl of Cumberland in an abortive attempt to relieve Sluys. In the intervals between these periods of activity he "kept company with the best" and became distinguished as a gay and gallant courtier. Again, although it may seem little connected with the sphere of his other activities, he sat in Parliament as Member for Morpeth from 1586-8, and again in 1593. In 1588 he eagerly seized the opportunity of assisting as a gentleman volunteer at the repulse of the Spanish Armada, his account of which is very graphic.

When the Earl of Essex was despatched to France with 4000 men for the assistance of Henry IV, Carey accompanied him and was present at the capture of Arques and the ineffective siege of Rouen. He indeed rendered that unfortunate favourite a yet greater service by returning to England and paving the way for a reconciliation between him and the Queen, for which he received the honour of Knighthood from the Earl's own hand in 1591. Of the subsequent fate of Essex, it is to be observed that he makes no mention.

His Marriage

In 1593 Carey took to wife Eliza, the widowed daughter of Sir Hugh Trevannion, a step at which the Queen was pleased to exhibit violent indignation. With a few vivid touches Sir Robert brings before us the "stormy and terrible encounter" in which his despotic relative "spoke her pleasure" – interspersed no doubt with her favourite expletives – of him and his wife.

He succeeded, however, in recovering her favour, with the ingenuity and address that he on more than one occasion exhibited.

His Wardenship of the Marches

It was at this period that (partly through the interest of Lord Scrope, who had married his sister, and partly in succession to his father, Lord Hunsdon) Carey began his career as "Warden of the Marches" where, during the last ten years of Elizabeth's reign, he accomplished what we may presume to have been the most serious work of his life.

This consisted in clearing the country of freebooters, and in the general pacification of the Marches. Of the means by which he achieved this result, we are told that he spent "few days not on horseback," and made the personal acquaintance of such local celebrities as "Geordie Bourne" and "Sim of the Calfhill," whose traits of character give so much colour to his pages. And the Almighty (he tells us) so blessed his labours, that he succeeded in capturing and hanging nearly a score of freebooters in a single summer.

Such enterprises as the great "drive" of Tarras Moss, which made Carey's Raid for ever famous in Liddesdale, present to us, at first hand, exactly that romantic atmosphere half sporting, half warlike, eternally associated with "The Border" in the pages of Scott. Another of Carey's experiences supplies an instructive parallel to the more tragic episode of "Chevy Chace." And we can scarcely read of the "40 good horses, and good men (gentlemen's sonnes) to ride them," that he maintained at Alnwick Abbey, without recalling the "nine and twenty knights of fame" and the "thirty steeds" that stood, equally ready for action, at Branksome Hall.

Carey and the Queen

Finding it expedient to pay a hurried visit to the English Court again in 1603, Carey was, at about that time, admitted to several intimate audiences with the Queen, of whose death, on March 24 of that year, he gives us many valuable details unrecorded, or inaccurately recorded, by other writers. There is some pathos, too, in the personal touches, as when the Queen called him to her side, grasped his hand and wrung it hard, saying: "No, Robin, I am not well," though Carey's own chief anxiety was as to the "wretched state" in which he "himself would be left," as he acutely felt, at her Majesty's death.

Doubtless, like Elizabeth's other courtiers, he cherished some real regard for his Mistress, but this was not allowed to interfere with his more material interests. While other courtiers "wished for wings," Carey – as one of his editors observes – jumped upon a horse. The unjustifiable and indecent haste with which he galloped to Holyrood in Edinburgh – at almost a breakneck pace – to announce the important news of his accession to the first king of "England, Scotland, France, and Ireland," has been the subject of severe reflections. Indeed Carey's entire relations with James I, and the persistent and undignified intrigues for "place," reflected in his memoirs, well illustrate the strange union of the romantic spirit with great worldly prudence, which appears to some extent characteristic of the age of Elizabeth.

The financial transactions of this period are not always easy to follow. When we read that Sir Robert, at the date of his marriage, possessed nothing but an annual pension of £100, and that his debts amounted to £1000, we can hardly regard his costly present to the Queen (of something like four years income) as anything but a promising speculation. It is true that his wife possessed a jointure of £500 a year. But they could hardly have relied upon such resources alone.

The Crown was then regarded, by many a brave and active spirit, as the legitimate fountain not only of honours but of profit, indeed of sustenance.

Accession of James I

Thus as Carey's "livelyhood" depended, as he tells us, almost entirely upon the Queen's life he exhibits a natural alarm for his material interests on the accession of James I.

Sir Robert lost his Wardenry and "the pay of 40 horse" (about £1000 per annum): and had to surrender Norham Castle – his chief source of income – to Lord Dunbar, in return, it is true, for the sum of £6000, and some hundreds more for the furniture and fittings.

In 1605, however, he was appointed to take charge of the young Prince Charles – an office somewhat at a discount, he confides to us, owing to the uncertainty of the Prince's health. It is gratifying, however, to note that Charles's health, if not his very life, was largely due to the affectionate and sensible attentions of Lady Carey, who had the personal custody of his Royal Highness (with a salary of £400 a year) from the age of four to eleven.

Her husband meanwhile secured the position, for which he claimed, with some reason, to be specially fitted, of Master of the Robes to the young Prince. Carey never boasts of his activity in the field – but he did think he knew something about the choice and fit of clothes! and in spite of much intrigue and jealousy, succeeded in holding this post as well as that of Lord Chamberlain.

From the account of the "Bedchamber" squabbles here fully recorded, it will be seen that he and many of his peers exhibited as much energy in providing for their families by means of places at Court, as in hunting down freebooters on the Marches, or "chasing brave adventures with a naked sword" on the Continent or the Spanish main.

Expedition to Spain

Carey's last active employment was to follow Prince Charles and the Duke of Buckingham on their wild expedition to Spain in March 1623. But after a month at Madrid he was persuaded to return on account of his age and failing health.

He was created Baron Leppington in 1622, and on the accession of Charles I received the Earldom of Monmouth and an estate of £500 a year. This he regarded as a satisfactory compensation for the surrender of his office of Lord Chamberlain. And at his death in 1639 he would probably have regarded the position of his family as fairly secure. Both Sir Robert and his wife had for some years occupied profitable offices. His eldest son Henry, a Knight of the Bath, had married Martha, eldest daughter of Sir Lionel Cranfield, afterwards Earl of Middlesex and Lord Treasurer of England. He succeeded his father in the Earldom of Monmouth, which became extinct on his death without male issue. Carey's only daughter Philadelphia married the son and heir of Lord Wharton.

Thomas, the second son, was also married and left two daughters, married respectively to Sir Henry Littleton, and John Mordaunt, Lord Avalon.

The memoirs, which begin, as has been said, with the year 1577, were probably put together early in King Charles' reign, about 1627.

Editions of the Memoirs

They were first published with notes and introduction by the Earl of Corke and Orrery (the owner of the manuscript) in 1759. (The Earl of Corke was the great-grandson of Lady Frances Cranfield, the youngest sister of Martha, mentioned above).

A second edition also appeared in 1759, and the work was reprinted by the firm of Constables, with a few corrections and additional illustrations (more especially of the passages concerning the Border) by Sir Walter Scott, in 1808.

The Ripping Yarns.com edition is based on the 1905 edition, with its preface by GH Powell.

The content of the memoirs is essentially unchanged for this new edition, except that I have split the memoirs into more manageable "chapters" with headings.

Ian H. Robertson, Findon, Aberdeenshire, 2005.

Robert Carey's Memoirs
1577 – 1625

Early Days

I had the happiness to be born of good parents: I was youngest of ten sons; they brought me up under tutors and governors, to give me learning and knowledge, but I must acknowledge my own weakness, I had not ability to profit much thereby. After I attained to the years of seventeen or thereabouts, Sir Thomas Layton was sent Ambassador from the Queen to the States first, and then to Don John of Austria: my father the Lord Hunsdon fitted me to go the journey with him; we were abroad almost all the winter: after we had been with the States at Brussels, we took leave, and went on our journey towards Don John; we found him at Luxembourg: the next day he removed towards Namur, and appointed our Ambassador to meet him at Mons in Hainault, which we did, and there had audience of him: we stayed but two days with him, and took our leave: after some time spent, in our return, at Brussels with the States, we returned to Dunkirk, and there took shipping for England; and in short time came to court, where we dispersed, every man as he liked best.

Shortly after this, Monsieur the King of France's brother came and remained in our court a good time. All the time of his being here, God so blessed me with means and abilities as I was ever one in every action that our court triumphs then produced: and they were such as the best wits and inventions in those days could devise to make the court glorious, and to entertain so great a guest. This Duke's stay here, was from Michaelmas to Christmas; then he went from hence to Flushing, and from thence to Antwerp, where he was created, by the States, Duke of Brabant with great solemnity: My Lord of Nottingham as Admiral, my Lord of Sussex Chamberlain of the Queen's household, and my father, being Governor of Berwick, were sent to convoy him over in three of the Queen's best ships. They brought him to Antwerp, and after the Duke was settled in his government, they took their leave, and came for England. My father left me there behind him to stay some time with Sir John

Norrice, who then was in Antwerp: and thence he appointed me to travel into France, and there to stay for a time until he should send for me back. I stayed at Antwerp from Shrovetide until Easter; then I took my journey from thence into France, and made no stay until I came to Paris, and there I stayed nine months: then upon an accident of some fear in England, that Englishmen should be ill dealt with in France, my father sent for me in all haste, to come away with all the speed I could for England: though very unwillingly, I obeyed, and came home about Christmas.

The summer after, I went with Mr. Secretary Walsingham into Scotland, he being sent thither Ambassador from her Majesty; it pleased the King at that time to take such a liking of me, as he wrote earnestly to the Queen at our return to give me leave to come back to him again, to attend on him at his court, assuring her Majesty I should not repent my attendance.

Her Majesty gave her consent; I went to Berwick with my father a while after with full resolution to go to him, being well provided of men, money, apparel, and horses; but my father was no sooner come to Berwick, and I ready to take my journey to the King, but a countermand was sent to my father from the Queen, straightly charging him to stay me, and not to suffer me to go into Scotland to the King.

My journey being thus stayed, I returned shortly after, with my father, to the court. The beginning of the spring after, Sluys was besieged, and my Lord of Essex stole from court with intent to get into Sluys, if he could: the queen sent me after him, commanding me to use the best means if I could find him, to persuade him to return to court. I made no long stay, but with all the speed I could, went after him; I found him at Sandwich, and with much ado I got him to return: as we were riding post back, I stayed a little behind him, and when he was out of sight, I returned to Sandwich. I left my Lord of Cumberland there, who had provided a small barque; and we made all the haste we could toward Sluys.

When we came right over Ostend, the water was so shallow we could not get in with our barque, we took our ship-boat, and rowed toward Ostend: we were no sooner come near the shore, but we were told that Sluys was yielded to the enemy that day: notwithstanding, we went ashore to Ostend, where I found my brother Edmund, a captain of the town. We were no sooner come to our lodging, but it was told us for certain that the enemy was fully resolved to besiege Ostend with the greatest expedition that they could. The next morning my Lord of Cumberland, seeing our hopes frustrate by the town's yielding, resolved to go to his barque again, and from Flushing to go to Bergen-op-Zoom to see my Lord of Leicester, and then to return home again, thinking that I would go with him: but I was resolved of another way, and told him that it was for certain reported that the enemy would shortly besiege the town, that I had a brother there, whom I could not leave; but meant to be partner with him both in good and ill. We took leave; he to his barque, and I to stay with my brother. The report increased daily more and more of the enemy's approach within two or three days after my Lord of Nottingham, that was our Admiral, came to us with provision of munition and victuals, and left with us Sir William Read to be commander of the town. After he had stayed two or three days with us, he took ship again, and went for England. We stayed there some fortnight. At last letters came to us from my Lord of Leicester, that the town that year was free from any siege, and commanded that six of the companies that were there should embark themselves with all speed, and come to him to Bergen-op-Zoom. We came the next day (for my brother's company being one of those were appointed to go, I went with him). I stayed there most part of the summer: many things in that time were attempted, nothing of worth performed. I, finding no hope of any good action to be performed, towards Michaelmas returned for England, and found by that little experience, that a brave war and a poor spirit in a commander never agree well together.

The next year (which was 1586) was the Queen of Scots' beheading. I lived in court, had small means of my friends: yet God so blessed me that I was ever able to keep company with the best: in all triumphs I was one; either at tilt, tourney, or barriers in masque or balls I kept men and horses far above my rank, and so continued a long time. At which time (few or none in the court being willing to undertake that journey) her Majesty sent me to the King of Scots, to make known her innocence of her sister's death, with letters of credence from herself to assure all that I should affirm.

I was waylaid in Scotland, if I had gone in, to have been murdered: but the King's Majesty, knowing the disposition of his people, and the fury they were in, sent to me to Berwick, to let me know that no power of his could warrant my life at that time; therefore to prevent further mischief, he would send me no convoy, but would send two of his Council to the boundary-road, to receive my letters, or what other message I had to deliver. I had reason to give his Majesty thanks, and so I did; and sent him word I would with all speed advertise her Majesty of the gracious care he had of me; and as I should be directed, I would inform his Majesty. I was commanded to accept of the King's offer. Sir George Hume, and the master of Melven, met me at the boundary-road, where I delivered my message in writing, and my letters from the Queen to the King; and then came presently (post) to court, where I had thanks of her Majesty for what I had done.

The next year (1587) I was sent Ambassador again to the King of Scots. When I came to Berwick, I sent for a safe conduct. I had word from the King, he was going a journey towards Lochmaben to suppress some rebels that held that castle against him, and therefore desired me to make what haste I could to Carlisle, and from thence I should come to him to Dumfries, and there he would warrant my safe coming and my safe return. I did as I was directed, and came to Dumfries, where I was by his Majesty nobly entertained; and stayed with him there some fourteen days, and then took my leave, and came for England: and by the way I sent to the King from Carlisle two pieces of ordnance, with bullets, powder, and all things necessary, by which means he recovered his castle. But Robert Maxfield that held the castle against him, made an escape, and got to sea, and so prevented the King's justice for that time. I returned to court, where the

Queen and Council allowed very well of what I had done; and so I ended that journey.

The Spanish Armada

The next year (1588) the King of Spain's great Armada came upon our coast, thinking to devour us all. Upon the news sent to court from Plymouth of their certain arrival, my Lord Cumberland and myself took post horse, and rode straight to Portsmouth, where we found a frigate that carried us to sea; and having sought for the fleets a whole day, the night after we fell amongst them: where it was our fortune to light first on the Spanish fleet; and finding ourselves in the wrong, we tacked about, and in short time got to our own fleet, which was not far from the other. At our coming aboard our Admiral, we stayed there awhile; but finding the ship much pestered, and scant of cabins, we left the Admiral, and went aboard Captain Reyman, where we stayed, and were very welcome, and much made of. It was on Thursday that we came to the fleet. All that day we followed close the Spanish Armada, and nothing was attempted on either side: the same course we held all Friday and Saturday, by which time the Spanish fleet cast anchor just before Calais. We likewise did the same, a very small distance behind them, and so continued till Monday morning about two of the clock; in which time our Council of war had provided six old hulks, and stuffed them full of all combustible matter fit for burning, and on Monday at two in the morning they were let loose, with each of them a man in her to direct them. The tide serving they brought them very near the Spanish fleet, so that they could not miss to come amongst the midst of them: then they set fire on them, and came off themselves, having each of them a little boat to bring him off. The ships set on fire, came so directly to the Spanish fleet, as they had no way to avoid them, but to cut all their hawsers, and so escape; and their haste was such that they left one of their four great galliasses on ground before Calais, which our men took and had the spoil of, where many of the Spaniards were slain with the Governor thereof, but most of them were saved with wading ashore to Calais. They being in this disorder, we made ready to follow them, where began a cruel fight, and we had such advantage both of wind and tide, as we had a glorious day of them; continuing fight from four o'clock in the morning, till almost five or six at night, where they lost a dozen or fourteen of their best ships, some sunk, and the rest ran ashore in divers parts to keep themselves from sinking. After God had given us this great victory, they made all the haste they could away, and we followed them Tuesday and Wednesday, by which time they were gotten as far as Flamborough Head. It was resolved on Wednesday at night, that by four o'clock on Thursday, we should have a new fight with them for a farewell; but by two in the morning, there was a flag of Council hung out in our Vice-Admiral, when it was found that in the whole fleet there was not munition sufficient to make half a fight; and therefore it was there concluded that we should let them pass, and our fleet to return to the Downs. That night we parted with them, we had a mighty storm.

Our fleet cast anchor, and endured it: but the Spanish fleets, wanting their anchors, were many of them cast ashore on the west of Ireland, where they had all their throats cut by the Kernes; and some of them on Scotland, where they were no better used: and the rest (with much ado) got into Spain again. Thus did God bless us, and gave victory over this invincible navy: the sea calmed, and all our ships came to the Downs on Friday in safety.

On Saturday my Lord of Cumberland and myself came on shore, and took post horse, and found the Queen in her army at Tilbury camp, where I fell sick of a burning fever, and was carried in a litter to London. I should have been then sent Ambassador to the King of Scots, but could not by reason of my sickness.

In France with Lord Essex

The next year (which was 1589) was the journey of Portugal, where my Lord of Essex stole from court to go that journey, and left me behind him, which did so much trouble me, that I had no mind to stay in the court; but having given out some money to go on foot in twelve days to Berwick, I performed it that summer, which was worth to me two thousand pounds, which bettered me to live at court a good while after.

The next journey I undertook was into France with my Lord of Essex. I was a Captain of one hundred and fifty men. This journey was very chargeable to me, for I carried with me a waggon with five horses to draw it, I carried five great horses over with me, and one little ambling nag, and I kept a table all the while I was there that cost me thirty pounds a week, which was from Midsummer to almost Christmas; and yet God so blessed me that I never wanted, but He still sent me means to supply my wants.

My Lord [of Essex] had over with him two hundred horse, and four thousand foot, besides volunteers which were many. After that my Lord had stayed at Arques beside Dieppe some three weeks, or more, and had commodiously lodged his army, he made a journey to Noyon, and passed still through the enemy's country, without any let or interruption, and took only his two hundred horse for his guard. In three long days' journey we came to the King to Noyon. There my Lord stayed with the King four days, and then returned towards Arques again: but in the return we might see many troops of horse of the enemy approaching very near us, but they never durst set upon us, so that we came in safety to Gisors, a garrison town of the King's. The next day we were to go to Arques, the way that we came. Our carriages were loaded and gone out of the ports of the town, and my Lord and his company were on horseback ready to follow; but there came a French gentleman in good time to the town, and stayed our carriages, and came in great haste to my Lord, and desired to speak with him in private; my Lord alighted, and went into his lodging with him, and most of the company stayed on horseback expecting his return.

When the Frenchman and my Lord were together, he discovered to my Lord that he was betrayed by the Governor of the town, and that by his intelligence Monsieur Villars with above two thousand foot, and five hundred horse, were laid in a great wood, some three miles off of the town which we were to pass through, to cut us all to pieces. This being made known to my Lord, some few of my Lord's friends were called to Council, and presently it was resolved that we should make no stay there, but turn our course towards Pont de l'Arche, so we marched a clean contrary way to that we should have done, and some nine miles off of the town, we put over the river Seine, and lay on the other side of the river in the open field all that night.

The next day we got betimes to Pont de l'Arche, where by the Governor of the town, my Lord and all his troops were very well entertained. By this means God so blessed us that we escaped this imminent danger. Being all safe at Pont de l'Arche, my Lord sent to Arques for all his foot to come to him, which came in five or six days. After they had rested awhile, he took leave of the Governor, and marched by small journeys towards Arques (for then we feared no encounter of any enemy). The second night we lodged at a great village-town called Pavilly, where finding great store of victuals, and all things necessary for the relief of the soldiers, it was resolved that we should stay there four or five days. In which time, to show Villars how little we esteemed him and his forces, in a morning betimes both foot and horse marched some five miles off, only in a bravado, to see whether Villars or any of his troops in the town durst come out and skirmish with us; but there unfortunately we lost Mr. Walter Devereux, my Lord's only brother, with a shot in the head, and so we returned that night to Pavilly, the whole army being full of sorrow for the loss of so worthy a gentleman.

The next night after, the town fell on fire, and in less than an hour it was all burnt to the ground, so that we had much ado to get our troops and carriages safe out of the town.

In four days after we came to Arques, where our horse and foot rested a good space and refreshed themselves, till it was resolved that my Lord and his troops only should go to besiege Gournay, which was some fortnight after. We had not stayed long at Arques, but the whole army removed from thence towards Gournay to besiege the town. We lay before it some ten days, in which time there came letters out of England to my Lord of Essex, to command him presently to repair for England, and to leave his charge with Sir Thomas Layton. He presently despatched Sir Thomas Darcy to desire longer stay; and to let the Queen know that the King intended shortly to besiege Rouen, and what a dishonour it would be for ever to him, if he should leave him at such a time. Here Colonel Cromwell left the camp, and went for England, having such urgent occasions of business that he could stay no longer. My Lord of Essex upon his departure gave me his regiment, and I made choice of my Lord of Valentia to be my Lieutenant-Colonel of my regiment, and gave my Captainship to Sir Francis Rich, who was Lieutenant of my company before. After we had battered the town, and made a breach, in a morning betimes we were ready to give an assault; but the chief commanders of the town, fearing their own weakness, held out a white flag to parley, and upon conference it was agreed, that the commanders and soldiers should in safety pass out of the town, and that the town should be delivered to my Lord for the King's use. All which was performed that morning before twelve of the clock.

From this town my Lord sent me to court with the news of the yielding of the town, and the manner of it. I made what haste I could to get over from Dieppe, and within four days after I left my Lord, I arrived at Oatlands betimes in the morning. Before I came, Sir Thomas Darcy was sent back with a straight command for my Lord to return, as he would answer it at his utmost peril, with commission for Sir Thomas Layton to execute the place. I spoke with most of the Council before the Queen was stirring, who assured me that there was no removing of her Majesty from her resolution, and advised me to take heed that I gave her no cause to be offended with me, by persuading her for his stay, which they assured me would do no good, but rather hurt. About ten of the clock she sent for me. I delivered her my

Lord's letter. She presently burst out into a great rage against my Lord, and vowed she would make him an example to all the world, if he presently left not his charge, and returned upon Sir Francis Darcy's coming to him. I said nothing to her till she had read his letter. She seemed to be meanly well contented with the success at Gournay, and then I said to her,

"Madam, I know my Lord's care is such to obey all your commands, as he will not make one hour's stay after Sir Francis hath delivered him his fatal doom; but, Madam, give me leave to let your Majesty know beforehand, what you shall truly find at his return, after he hath had the happiness to see you, and kiss your hand. He doth so sensibly feel his disgrace, and however you think it reason for this you have done, yet the world abroad who know not the cause of his so sudden leaving his army to another, will esteem it a weakness in him, and a base cowardliness in him to leave the army, now, when he should meet the King and his whole army for the besieging of Rouen. You will be deceived, Madam, if you think he will ever after this have to do with court or state affairs. I know his full resolution is to retire to some cell in the country, and to live there, as a man never desirous to look a good man in the face again. And in good faith, Madam, to deal truly with your Majesty, I think you will not have him a long-lived man after his return. The late loss of his brother, whom he loved so dearly, and this heavy doom that you have laid upon him, will in a short time break his heart. Then your Majesty will have sufficient satisfaction for the offence he hath committed against you."

She seemed to be something offended at my discourse, and bade me go to dinner. I desired her that if she pleased to command me any service, I might know her pleasure in the afternoon, for I meant with all the haste I could make to return to my charge. I had scarce made an end of my dinner, but I was sent for to come to her again. She delivered me a letter, written with her own hand to my Lord, and bade me tell him, that "if there were anything in it that did please him, he should give me thanks for it." I humbly kissed her hand, and said to her, "I hoped there was in it that which would make him of the most dejected man living, a new creature, rejoicing in nothing so much as that he had to serve so worthy and so gracious a mistress."

After I had with all due respects taken my leave of her, I made no long stay, but that afternoon I took post horse, and made for France. Thus God blessed me in this journey, that through my poor weakness I procured that from her which all my Lord's friends in court, nor all her Council could procure.

I made all the haste I could, but came too late, for that tide that I came to the haven to Dieppe, my Lord having received her straight command from Sir Francis Darcy, resigned his charge to Sir Thomas Layton, and put himself into a little skiff in Dieppe, and made all the haste he could for England. When I came to Dieppe, they all wondered that I missed him, for they told me it was not two hours since he set sail from thence. Missing him I went to my charge at Arques, and there stayed till my Lord's return. At my Lord's coming to court, whereas he expected nothing but her Majesty's heavy displeasure he found it clean contrary, for she used him with that grace and favour, that he stayed a week with her, passing the time in jollity and feasting; and then with tears in her eyes, she showed her affection to him, and for the repair of his honour gave him leave to return to his charge again.

He made all the haste he could to Dieppe. I met him there. As soon as he saw me he drew his rapier, and came running to me, and laid it on my shoulder, and straightly embraced me, and said to me, when he had need of one to plead for him, he would never use any other orator than myself. I delivered him the Queen's letter, then he said, "Worthy cousin, I know by herself how you prevailed with her, and what a true friend I had of you, which I shall never forget."

The next day my Lord went to Arques, and there we stayed till we took our journey to Rouen. In short time after my Lord coming to his army at Arques (where there was no small joy for his Lordship's safe return) he received from the King his resolution what day and time he (Henry IV) meant to besiege the city of Rouen with his whole army both horse and foot; and desired my Lord to fit himself and his troops at the time appointed, which he slacked not to perform with all care and diligence.

My Lord's quarter was allotted to be at Mount Malade, the town lying under us not full a quarter of an English mile. The King with his horse and foot, took for his quarter the town of Darnetal. Between the King and my Lord lay the Switzers, upon another hill. Upon the right hand of my Lord lay Montmorency, close to the town on low ground; the rest of the King's army, as well on the side we lay on, as on the other side of the water, were dispersed in divers parts. Monsieur de Roulet (Governor of Pont de l'Arche) with his troops, were lodged on the other side of the water. The rest of the commanders and the names of the places they lay in, I do not well remember, but sure I am, my Lord came to his quarter by five o'clock in the morning, and the whole town was roundly besieged before eleven of the clock. But Villars, Governor of Rouen, did that day show himself to be a brave soldier, and a great commander. He brought out his troops both of horse and foot, and there was not a quarter in the whole army but what was bravely assaulted and fought withal by them that day. The King's quarter was not exempted; but they did so furiously assault Montmorency's quarter, that had not my Lord of Essex sent his horse to relieve him, he had been driven out of his quarter with great dishonour. Towards three in the afternoon they had shown their worth and valour in all other places. They came up towards my Lord's quarters. We were ready to entertain them, and we held skirmish at the least two hours, and after some killed and hurt on both sides, they fairly retired into the town, and we to our lodging; and so ended that day's sport.

Divers days after, they made sallies out of the town, and gave attempts to divers quarters, which we that lay on high had the pleasure to behold, but they never attempted anything against us but the first day. They had a spleen to no quarter so much as to Montmorency's. The reason for that was he had begged of the King the government of the town, if it had been taken either by agreement or by assault.

We lay long there and to little purpose; for though the town walls were weak, and of no force to endure a battery, which my Lord would fain have been at, and offered the King that he and his troops should be the first that should enter, if he would make a breach (which four cannons would soon have done), it would not be hearkened unto; old Biron thinking it better by continuing the siege, for want of victuals to make them come to composition, than to hazard the wealth of the town to the spoil of the soldiers, if it should be won by assault.

All our attempts were against St. Katherine's. There we wrought in trenches so near them, as we came to lie in their counterscarp, and had often conference with them in the fort. One night there were scaling ladders prepared, and we had hope to win it by escalade. My Lord was there with the chief gentlemen of his army. We were all commanded to wear shirts above the armour (I lost many shirts that I lent that night); this was done accordingly. When all things were prepared and ready, we marched forwards, and the first that came to set up the ladders found them (at least) two yards too short; so we were forced to retire with shame enough, the fort playing upon us in our coming on, and in our coming off, but there was little hurt done by reason of the darkness of the night.

One day my Lord and his best friends being at the head of the French prattling to those in the fort, we had been all cut in pieces had not the worth and valour of Sir Ferdinando George prevented it by God's assistance. For he having charge of the trenches that day, and a Corps of English Guards by him, it was God's will that he, looking through a loophole, espied twenty-five or thirty armed men with halberds sallying out of the fort, who meant to come upon us on a sudden by a by-way that they had, and to cut all our throats but he on a sudden (seeing the present danger) by commanding a dozen or fourteen of his best soldiers whom he trusted most to follow him in his doublet and hose, and his rapier by his side, leapt over the trenches, the rest bravely following him, and with all speed came upon them that were coming to this execution. They seeing this desperate resolution (whether they thought they had been betrayed, or what else I know not) retired into the fort with all speed back again, and he came bravely off with all his followers without any hurt, though they had many shots made at them in their going on and coming off from the ramparts. Thus by God's help, and this man's brave resolution, my Lord and all that were with him escaped this eminent danger.

All the attempts we made were only against the fort, my Lord still urging the King to batter some part of the town, but it would never be yielded to. Thus we spent a long time to little purpose, from Michaelmas to almost Christmas, when the Duke of Parma came with an army to relieve the town, and did effect it.

The King was forced to raise his siege with shame enough, and to retire: at which time the winter coming on, my Lord left his army with Sir Roger Williams, Sir Thomas Baskerville, and other commanders, took his leave of the King, and came for England.

I returned with my Lord, and left my regiment with Sir Henry Power (now Viscount Valentia) and some fortnight before Christmas my Lord and those that came with him arrived at court, where he was very welcome to the Queen and all that attended him, for his sake. Thus ended our French wars.

First Actions on the Scottish Border

I spent two winters and a summer in court after this, in which time the Queen gave me out of the Exchequer one thousand pounds to pay my debts, which gave me great relief. Presently after this, my old Lord Scrope died at Carlisle, and the Queen gave the West Wardenry to his son that had married my sister. He having that office imposed upon him, came to me with great earnestness, and desired me to be his deputy, offering me yearly that I should live with him in his house, he would allow me half a dozen men, and as many horses, to be kept at his charge; and his fee being a thousand marks yearly, he would part it with me, and I should have the half. This his noble offer I accepted of, left the court, and went with him to Carlisle, where I was no sooner come but I entered into my office.

Thus after I had passed my best time in court, and got little, I betook myself to the country, after I was past one and thirty years old, where I lived with great content: for we had a stirring world, and few days passed over my head but I was on horseback, either to prevent mischief; or to take malefactors, and to bring the border in better quiet than it had been in times past. God blessed me in all my actions, and I cannot remember that I undertook anything in the time that I was there but it took good effect. One memorable thing of God's mercy showed unto me, was such, as I have good cause still to remember it.

I had private intelligence given me that there were two Scottish men that had killed a churchman in Scotland, and were by one of the Greenes relieved. This Greene dwelt within five miles of Carlisle; he had a pretty house, and close by it a strong tower for his own defence in time of need. I thought to surprise the Scots on a sudden, and about two o'clock in the morning I took horse in Carlisle, and not above twenty-five in my company, thinking to surprise the house on a sudden. Before I could surround the house, the two Scots were gotten into the strong tower, and I might see a boy riding from the house as fast as his horse could carry him, I little suspecting what it meant: but

Thomas Carleton came to me presently, and told me that if I did not presently prevent it, both myself and all my company would be either slain or taken prisoners. It was strange to me to hear this language. He then said to me, "Do you see that boy that rideth away so fast he will be in Scotland within this half-hour, and he is gone to let them know that you are here, and to what end you are come, and the small number you have with you, and that if they will make haste, on a sudden they may surprise us, and do with us what they please."

Hereupon we took advice what was best to be done. We sent notice presently to all parts to raise the country, and to come to us with all the speed they could; and withal we sent to Carlisle to raise the townsmen, for without foot we could do no good against the tower. There we stayed some hours expecting more company, and within short time after, the country came in on all sides, so that we were quickly between three and four hundred horse; and after some little longer stay, the foot of Carlisle came to us to the number of three hundred or four hundred men; whom we set presently at work to get up to the top of the tower, and to uncover the roof, and then some twenty of them to fall down together, and by that means to win the tower. The Scots seeing their present danger offered to parley, and yielded themselves to my mercy.

They had no sooner opened the iron gate, and yielded themselves my prisoners, but we might see four hundred horse within a quarter of a mile coming to their rescue, and to surprise me and my small company: but of a sudden they stayed, and stood at gaze. Then I had more to do than ever, for all our borderers came crying with full mouths, "Sir, give us leave to set upon them, for these are they that have killed our fathers, our brothers, our uncles, and our cousins, and they are come thinking to surprise you, upon weak grass nags, such as they could get on a sudden, and God hath put them into your hands, that we may take revenge of them for much blood that they have spilt of ours."

I desired they would be patient awhile, and bethought myself; if I should give them their wills, there would be few or none of them (the Scots) that would escape unkilled (there was so many deadly feuds among them) and therefore I resolved with myself; to give them a fair answer, but not to give them their desire. So I told them that if I were not there myself, they might then do what pleased themselves, but being present, if I should give them leave, the blood that should be spilt that day would lie very heavy upon my conscience, and therefore I desired them for my sake to forbear, and if the Scots did not presently make away with all the speed they could upon my sending to them, they should then have their wills to do what they pleased. They were ill satisfied with my answer, but durst not disobey. I sent with speed to the Scots, and bade them pack away with all the speed they could, for if they stayed the messenger's return, they should few of them return to their own home. They made no stay, but they were turned homewards before the messenger had made an end of his message. Thus by God's mercy I escaped a great danger, and by my means there was a great many men's lives saved that day.

Marriage and the Queen's Disapproval

Not long after this I married a gentlewoman more for her worth than her wealth, for her estate was but five hundred pounds a year jointure, and she had between five and six hundred pounds in her purse. Neither did she marry me for any great wealth, for I had in all the world, but one hundred pounds a year pension out of the Exchequer, and that was but during pleasure, and I was near a thousand pounds in debt; besides, the Queen was mightily offended with me for marrying, and most of my best friends, only my father was no ways displeased at it, which gave me great content.

After I was married, I brought my wife to Carlisle, where we were so nobly used by my Lord that myself; my wife, and all my servants were lodged in the castle, where we lived with him, and had our diet for ourselves, our servants and horses, provided for as his own were. We had not long lived thus, but a sudden occasion called me up to the term, which then was at St. Albans, by reason of a great plague that year at London, the Queen lying then at Windsor. The cause was as follows:

There was an old gentleman in Suffolk that had an old wife, his name was Gardiner. They were childless. This man in recompense of some favour my father had done him (after his own life and his wife's) made an estate of a Lordship of his called Columbine Hall in Suffolk, to my brother William and his heirs male, and for want thereof to me and my heirs male, and for want thereof to my father and his heirs for ever.

My brother marries, and by fraudulent means, privately cuts me off from the entail, and by the consent of Gardiner and his wife, makes his own wife a jointure of this Lordship. My brother dies without children. Then came it out that this land was given in jointure to his wife. I commenced suit of law with her, my eldest brother took her part, by reason that if she had prevailed, after her life, the law had cast the land upon him. My sister-in-law and I had proceeded so far in Chancery, that the cause was to be heard and decided that Michaelmas term at St. Albans. Those that I put in trust to follow my law business wrote to me in plain words, that neither they nor anybody else durst follow the cause, they were so bitterly threatened by my brother's agent, who did assure them my brother would be there himself; to see that his sister-in-law should have no wrong, and then they should see who durst appear to contradict him. Thus did my brother by his power, mean to overthrow my right in my absence; for he assured himself I durst not come near the court, having so lately offended the Queen, and the most of my friends by my marriage. But he was deceived, for I having heard this by my servant that I put in trust to follow my business, I presently resolved to come to St. Albans, and to do my best to defend my own cause. I had not been there two days, but in the lodging where I lay, my brother's man came in to take up a lodging for his master. I asked him where my brother was? He told me he was within two miles of the town, and was come expressly out of the Isle of Wight, for no other cause but a business in law, wherein he made sure account to overthrow his adversary that term; but against whom it was he knew not. He took horse again, after he had provided a lodging, to meet his master. He met him not a mile from the town, and told him that he had found me there, and that I lay in the same house that he was to lie in. My brother at this news was much troubled, and stood musing with himself a good space; at last, of a sudden he turned his horse's head, and came not at all to St. Albans, but went to Windsor, and trusted others to follow the cause. My cause was so just that I ended the business that term, overthrew my sister's jointure, and had the land settled as it was *in statu quo prius*.

Having ended my business I meant to return to Carlisle again. My father wrote to me from Windsor that the Queen meant to have a great triumph there, on her coronation day, and that there was great preparation making for the course of the field and tourney. He gave me notice of the Queen's anger for my marriage, and said it may be, I being so near, and to return without honouring her day, as I ever before had done, might be a cause of her further dislike, but left it to myself to do what I thought best. My business of law therefore being ended, I came to court, and lodged there very privately, only I made myself known to my father and some few friends besides. I here took order and sent to London to provide me things necessary for the triumph: I prepared a present for her Majesty, which with my caparisons cost me above four hundred pounds. I came into the triumph unknown of any. I was the forsaken knight that had vowed solitariness, but hearing of this great triumph thought to honour my mistress with my best service, and then to return to pay my wonted mourning. The triumph ended, and all things well passed over to the Queen's liking. I then made myself known in court, and for the time I stayed there was daily conversant with my old companions and friends, but it so fell out that I made no long stay there: it was upon this occasion.

My brother Sir John Carey, that was then Marshal of Berwick, was sent to by the King of Scots to desire him that he would meet his Majesty at the boundary-road at a day appointed; for that he had a matter of great importance to acquaint his sister the Queen of England withal, but he would not trust the Queen's Ambassador with it, nor any other, unless it were my father, or some of his children. My brother sent him word he would gladly wait on his Majesty, but durst not until he had acquainted the Queen therewith, and when he had received her answer, he would acquaint him with it. My brother sent notice to my father of the King's desire. My father showed the letter to the Queen. She was not willing that my brother should stir out of the town, but knowing (though she would not know) that I was in court, she said, "I hear your fine son that has lately married so worthily, is hereabouts; send him if you will to know the King's pleasure." My father answered, he knew I would be glad to obey her commands. "No (said she) do you bid him go, for I have nothing to do with him." My father came and told me what had passed between them. I thought it hard to be sent, and not to see her, but my father told me plainly, that she would neither speak with me nor see me. "Sir," said I, "if she be on such hard terms with me, I had need be wary what I do. If I go to the King without her licence, it were in her power to hang me at my return, and for anything I see, it were ill trusting her." My father merrily went to the Queen, and told her what I said. She answered, "If the gentleman be so mistrustful, let the Secretary make a safe conduct to go and come, and I will sign it." Upon these terms I parted from court, and made all the haste for Scotland. I stayed but one night with my wife at Carlisle, and then to Berwick, and so to Edinburgh, where it pleased the King to use me very graciously; and after three or four days spent in sport and merriment, he acquainted me with what he desired the Queen should know; which when I understood, I said to his Majesty, "Sir, between subject and subject, a message may be sent and delivered without any danger; between two so great monarchs as your Majesty and my Mistress, I dare not trust my memory to be a relater, but must desire you would be pleased to write your mind to her. If you shall think fit to trust me with it, I shall faithfully discharge the trust reposed in me." He liked the notion, and said it should be so, and accordingly I had my despatch within four days.

I made all the haste I could to court, which was then at Hampton Court. I arrived there on St. Stephen's Day in the afternoon. Dirty as I was, I came into the presence, where I found the lords and ladies dancing. The Queen was not there.

My father went to the Queen, to let her know that I was returned. She willed him to take my message or letters, and bring them to her. He came for them, but I desired him to excuse me; for that which I had to say either by word or by writing, I must deliver myself. I could neither trust him, nor much less any other therewith. He acquainted her Majesty with my resolution. With much ado I was called for in; and I was left alone with her. Our first encounter was stormy and terrible, which I passed over with silence. After she had spoken her pleasure of me and my wife, I told her, that "She herself was the fault of my marriage, and that if she had but graced me with the least of her favours, I had never left her nor her court; and seeing she was the chief cause of my misfortune, I would never off my knees till I had kissed her hand, and obtained my pardon." She was not displeased with my excuse, and before we parted we grew good friends. Then I delivered my message and my papers, which she took very well, and at last gave me thanks for the pains I had taken. So having her princely word that she had pardoned and forgotten all faults, I kissed her hand, and came forth to the presence, and was in the court, as I was ever before.

This God did for me to bring me in favour with my sovereign; for if this occasion had been slipped, it may be I should never, never, have seen her face more.

After I had stayed all Christmas till almost Shrovetide, I took leave of her Majesty, and all the rest of my friends, and made straight for Carlisle. I continued there till the middle of May, still busying myself with the affairs of the borders, at which time my wife was brought to bed of a daughter.

Shortly after some of my Lord Scrope's officers were at a difference with me about border causes. My Lord (as I conceived) was more favourable on their sides than mine, whereupon I resolved not to continue his deputy any longer. We parted on very good terms, and about six weeks after my daughter was born, my wife and I took our leave of him, and came to Witherington, which was her jointure. There we stayed till towards the spring the next year, and having no employment, I resolved to repair again to the court.

My wife was by this time again with child. We set out from Witherington, and by easy journeys we got to London. My father having the keeping of Arundell House, I got lodging in it for myself, my wife, and my servants. I went daily to court, and passed the time as merrily as I had done before. I had not been there long but I was a suitor to my father for the reversion of Norham Castle, which he willingly granted, so I could get the Queen's consent. After I understood his pleasure, I proceeded no further in it till I had written to my brother John, who was Marshal of Berwick, for his goodwill, who had then one hundred pounds of mine out of the demesnes of Norham, as a gift from my father. He, when he understood my meaning, did what he could to hinder me of it, and made his means to old Burleigh, who moved the Queen not to grant the reversion without my brother's consent. He wrought so with her as her answer to me was, that till I had satisfied my brother John she would not grant my suit. I knew it was to no purpose to deal any further in it till I had spoken with my brother, and given him satisfaction to his content, and therefore deferred it till I returned to the north. By this time my wife grew something big, and by reason she could not well agree with the air of London, I went with her to a place called Denham, hard by Uxbridge, and there she stayed till she was brought to bed of a boy, which was about the middle of January.

Wardenship of the East March

Not long after this, Sir John Selby, who was Deputy Warden for my father of the East March, died, and then my father called me to him, and told me if I would accept the place, he would put me in possession of Norham; paying to my brother one hundred pounds per annum as he had done before. I willingly accepted his offer, and prepared myself for the journey, and left my wife and her children at Denham till she had gathered more strength, and was fit for travel. The first thing I did, was to agree with my brother for his goodwill for Norham, which I bought at a dear rate, for I continued to pay him one hundred pounds a year as long as he continued Marshal of Berwick, and besides I gave him my interest of a lease which was worth six hundred pounds a year, which should have fallen to me if I had survived him. Having perfected this agreement, my brother acquainted my Lord Treasurer therewithal. When the Queen knew thereof; she was pleased to grant me the reversion of the Captainship of Norham after my father's death, who had given me the possession of it in his lifetime.

Having thus ended with my brother, I then began to think of the charge I had taken upon me, which was the government of the East March in my father's absence. I wrote to Sir Robert Kerr, who was my opposite warden, a brave, active young man, and desired him that he would appoint a day when he and myself might privately meet in some part of the border, to take some good order for the quieting the borders, until my return from London, which journey I was shortly of necessity to take. He stayed my man all night, and wrote to me back that he was glad to have the happiness to be acquainted with me, and did not doubt but the country would be the better governed by our good agreements. I wrote to him on the Monday, and the Thursday after he appointed the place and hour of meeting.

After he had filled my man with drink, and put him to bed, he and some half a score with him got to horse, and came into England to a little village. There he broke up a house, and took out a poor fellow, who (he pretended) had done him some wrong, and before the door cruelly murdered him, and so came quietly home and went to bed. The next morning he delivered my man a letter in answer to mine, and returned him to me. It pleased me well at the reading of his kind letter, but when I heard what *a brave* he had put upon me, I quickly resolved what to do, which was, never to have to do with him until I was righted for the great wrong he had done me. Upon this resolution, the day I should have met with him, I took post, and with all the haste I could, rode to London, leaving him to attend my coming to him as was appointed. There he stayed from one till five, but heard no news of me. Finding by this that I had neglected him, he returned home to his house, and so things rested (with great dislike the one of the other) till I came back, which was with all the speed I could, my business being ended.

The first thing I did after my return, was to ask justice for the wrong he had done me, but I could get none. The borderers seeing our disagreement, thought the time wished for of them was come. The winter being begun there was raids made out of Scotland into the East March, and goods were taken three or four times a week. I had no other means left to quiet them, but still sent out of the garrison horsemen of Berwick to watch in the fittest places for them, and it was their good hap many times to light upon them with the stolen goods driving before them. They were no sooner brought before me, but a jury went upon them, and being found guilty they were presently hanged. A course which had been seldom used, but I had no way to keep the country quiet but to do so; for when the Scotch thieves found what a sharp course I took with them that were found with the bloody hand, I had in a short time the country more quiet. All this while we were but in jest as it were, but now began the great quarrel between us.

There was a favourite of his, a great thief: called Geordie Bourne. This gallant, with some of his associates, would in a bravery come and take goods in the East March. I had that night some of the garrison abroad. They met with this Geordie and his fellows, driving of cattle before them. The garrison set upon them, and with a shot killed Geordie Bourne's uncle, and he himself, bravely resisting till he was sore hurt in the head, was taken. After he was taken, his pride was such that he asked, who it was who durst avow that night's work but when he heard it was the garrison, he was then more quiet.

But so powerful and awful was this Sir Robert Kerr and his favourites, as there was not a gentleman in all the East March that durst offend them. Presently after he was taken, I had most of the gentlemen of the March come to me, and told me, that now I had the ball at my foot, and might bring Sir Robert Kerr to what condition I pleased, for that this man's life was so near and dear unto him, as I should have all that my heart could desire for the good and quiet of the country and myself; if upon any condition I would give him his life. I heard them and their reasons, notwithstanding I called a jury the next morning, and he was found guilty of March-treason. Then they feared that I would cause him to be executed that afternoon which made them come flocking to me, humbly entreating me that I would spare his life till the next day, and if Sir Robert Kerr came not himself to me, and made me not such proffers as I could not but accept, that then I should do with him what I pleased. And further they told me plainly, that if I should execute him before I had heard from Sir Robert Kerr, they must be forced to quit their houses and fly the country; for his fury would be such against me and the March I commanded, as he would use all his power and strength to the utter destruction of the East March. They were so earnest with me, that I gave them my word he should not die that day. There was post upon post sent to Sir Robert Kerr, and some of them rode to him themselves to advertise him in what danger Geordie Bourne was: how he was condemned, and should have been executed that afternoon, but by their humble suit I gave them my word, that he should not die that day; and therefore besought him that he would send to me with all the speed he could to let me know that he would be the next day with me, to offer me good conditions for the safety of his life.

When all things were quiet and the watch set at night, after supper about ten of the clock, I took one of my men's liveries and put it about me, and took two other of my servants with me in their liveries, and we three as the Warden's men came to the Provost Marshal's where Bourne was, and were let into his chamber. We sat down by him, and told him that we were desirous to see him, because we heard he was stout and valiant, and true to his friend; and that we were sorry our master could not be moved to save his life. He voluntarily of himself said, that he had lived long enough to do so many villainies as he had done, and withal told us that he had lain with above forty men's wives, what in England, what in Scotland; and that he had killed seven Englishmen with his own hands, cruelly murdering them: that he had spent his whole time in whoring, drinking, stealing, and taking deep revenge for slight offences. He seemed to be very penitent, and much desired a minister for the comfort of his soul. We promised him to let our master know his desire, who, we knew, would presently grant it. We took our leave of him, and presently I took order that Mr. Selby, a very worthy honest preacher, should go to him, and not stir from him till his execution the next morning for after I had heard his own confession, I was resolved no conditions should save his life; and so took order that at the gates opening the next morning, he should be carried to execution, which accordingly was performed.

The next morning I had one from Sir Robert Kerr for a parley, who was within two miles staying for me. I sent him word "I would meet him where he pleased, but I would first know upon what terms and conditions." Before his man was returned he had heard, that in the morning very early Geordie Bourne had been executed. Many vows he made of cruel revenge, and returned home full of grief and disdain, and from that time forward still plotted revenge. He knew the gentlemen of the country were altogether sacklesse, and to make open raid upon the March would but show his malice, and lay him open to the punishment due to such offences. But his practice was how to be revenged on me or some of mine.

It was not long after that my brother and I had intelligence that there was a great match made at football, and the chief riders were to be there. The place they were to meet at was Shelsy, and that day we heard it, was the day for the meeting. We presently called a council, and after much dispute it was concluded, that the likeliest place he was to come to, was to kill the scouts. And it was the more suspected, for that my brother before my coming to the office, for cattle stolen out of the bounds, and as it were from under the walls of Berwick, being refused justice (upon his complaint) or at least delayed, sent of the garrison into Liddesdale, and killed there the chief offender which had done the wrong.

Upon this conclusion, there was order taken that both horse and foot should lie in ambush in divers parts of the bounds to defend the scouts, and to give a sound blow to Sir Robert and his company. Before the horse and foot were set out with directions what to do, it was almost dark night, and the gates ready to be locked. We parted, and I was by myself coming to my house; God put it into my mind, that it might well be, he meant destruction to my men that I had sent out to gather tithes for me at Norham, and their rendezvous was every night to lie and sup at an alehouse in Norham. I presently caused my page to take horse, and to ride as fast as his horse could carry him, and to command my servants (which were in all, eight), that presently upon his coming to them they should all change their lodging, and go straight to the castle, there to lie that night in straw and hay. Some of them were unwilling thereto, but durst not disobey; so all together left their alehouse, and retired to the castle. They had not well settled themselves to sleep, but they heard in the town a great alarm; for Sir Robert and his company came straight to the alehouse, broke open the doors, and made inquiry for my servants. They were answered, that by my command they were all in the castle. After they had searched all the house and found none, they feared they were betrayed, and with all the speed they could made haste homewards again. Thus God blessed me from this bloody tragedy.

All the whole March expected nightly some hurt to be done; but God so blessed me and the government I held, as, for all his (Sir Robert Kerr's) fury, he never drew drop of blood in all my March, neither durst his thieves trouble it much with stealing, for fear of hanging if they were taken. Thus we continued a year, and then God sent a means to bring things to better quiet by this occasion.

There had been commissioners in Berwick chosen by our Queen and the King of Scots, for the better quieting of the borders. By their industry they found a great number of malefactors guilty, both in England and Scotland; and they took order that the officers of Scotland should deliver such offenders as were guilty in their jurisdictions to the opposite officers in England, to be detained prisoners, till they had made satisfaction for the goods they had taken out of England. The like order was taken with the Wardens of England, and days prefixed for the delivery of them all. And in case any of the officers on either side should omit their duties, in not delivering the prisoners at the days and places appointed, that then there should a course be taken by the sovereigns, that what chief officer soever should offend herein, he himself should be delivered and detained till he had made good what the commissioners had agreed upon.

The English officers did punctually at the day and place deliver their prisoners, and so did most of the officers of Scotland, only the Lord of Buccleugh and Sir Robert Kerr were faulty. They were complained of, and new days appointed for the delivery of their prisoners. Buccleugh was the first that should deliver, and he failing entered himself prisoner into Berwick, there to remain till those officers under his charge were delivered to free him. He chose for his guardian Sir William Selby, Master of the Ordnance at Berwick. When Sir Robert Kerr's day of delivery came he failed too, and my Lord Hume, by the King's command, was to deliver him prisoner into Berwick upon the like terms, which was performed. Sir Robert Kerr (contrary to all men's expectation) chose me for his guardian, and home I brought him to my own house, after he delivered to me. I lodged him as well as I could, and took order for his diet and men to attend on him, and sent him word, that (although by his harsh carriage towards me, ever since I had that charge, he could not expect any favour, yet) hearing so much goodness of him that he never broke his word, if he would give me his hand and credit to be a true prisoner, he should have no guard set upon him, but have free liberty for his friends in Scotland to have ingress and regress to him as often as he pleased. He took this very kindly at my hands, accepted of my offer, and sent me thanks.

Some four days passed; all which time his friends came unto him, and he kept his chamber. Then he sent to me, and desired me I would come and speak with him, which I did; and after long discourse, charging and recharging one another with wrong and injuries, at last, before our parting, we became good friends, with great protestations on his side never to give me occasion of unkindness again. After our reconciliation he kept his chamber no longer, but dined and supped with me. I took him abroad with me, at the least thrice a week, a hunting, and every day we grew better friends. Buccleugh in few days after had his pledges delivered, and was set at liberty. But Sir Robert Kerr could not get his, so that I was commanded to carry him to York, and there to deliver him prisoner to the Archbishop, which accordingly I did. At our parting he professed great love to me for the kind usage I had shown him, and that I should find the effects of it upon his delivery, which he hoped would be shortly.

Thus we parted; and not long after his pledges were got, and brought to York, and he set at liberty. After his return home, I found him as good as his word. We met often at days or truce, and I had as good justice as I could desire; and so we continued very kind and good friends all the time that I stayed in that March, which was not long.

For presently after this my father died, and I had letters sent down from Secretary Cecil that it was her Majesty's pleasure I should continue as absolute Warden in my father's place, until her further pleasure were known. I continued so about a twelvemonth, and lived at my own charge, which impaired my poor estate very much. In this time God sent me another son, which was born and christened at Berwick. I did often solicit Mr. Secretary for some allowance to support me in my place, but could get no direct answer. I sued for leave to come up myself, but could get none. The March was very quiet, and all things in good order, and I adventured without leave to come up.

The Queen lay at Theobalds, and early in a morning I came thither. I first went to Mr. Secretary, who was much troubled when he saw me, and by no means could I get him to let the Queen know that I was there, but counselled me to return, that she might never know what I had done. When I could do no good with him, I went to my brother, who then was Chamberlain, after my Lord Cobham's death. I found him far worse than the other; and I had no way to save myself from some great disgrace, but to return without her knowledge of my being there; for by no entreaty could I get him to acquaint her with it. I was much troubled, and knew not well what to do. The Queen went that day to dinner to Enfield House, and had toils set up in the park to shoot at bucks, after dinner. I durst not be seen by her, these two Councillors had so terrified me. But after dinner I went to Enfield, and walking solitary in a very private place, exceeding melancholy, it pleased God to send Mr. William Killigrew, one of the privy chamber, to pass by where I was walking, who saluted me very kindly, and bade me welcome. I answered him very kindly, and he, perceiving me very sad, and something troubled, asked me why I was so. I told him the reason. He made little reckoning of what they had said to me, but bade me comfort myself for he would go presently to the Queen, and tell her of my coming up, on such a fashion as he did warrant me she would take it well, and bid me welcome. Away he went, and I stayed for his return. He told the Queen that she was more beholden to one man than to many others that made greater show of their love and service. She was desirous to know who it was. He told her it was myself, who, not having seen her for a twelve-month and more, could no longer endure to be deprived of so great a happiness, but took post with all speed to come up to see your Majesty, and to kiss your hand, and so to return instantly again. She presently sent him back for me, and received me with more grace and favour than ever she had done before; and after I had been with her a pretty while she was called for to go to her sports. She arose, I took her by the arm, and led her to her standing. My brother and Mr. Secretary seeing this thought it more than a miracle. She continued her favour to me the time I stayed, which was not long; for she took order I should have five hundred pounds out of the Exchequer for the time I had served, and I had a patent given me under the great seal to be her Warden of the East March. And thus was I preserved by a pretty jest, when wise men thought I had wrought my own wreck. For out of weakness God can show strength, and His goodness was never wanting to me in any extremity.

With grace and favour I returned to my charge again: yet before my return the Queen was pleased to renew my grant of Norham, with the life of both my sons, and the longer liver of us. I was not long settled in my office but there fell out a new occasion to remove me; which was, that my Lord of Willoughby (who was newly come from travel) was made Governor of Berwick, and the East March did properly belong to the Governor there. He came down with full commission for both places, so that I was now to seek what course of life to take. Being at liberty up came I to court, where long I did not stay; but new occasion was offered me to continue a Northern man still.

Sir John Foster, who had been an active and valiant man, and had done great good service in the Middle March (of which place he had been long Warden), grew at length to that weakness by reason of his age, that the borderers knowing it grew insolent, and by reason of their many excursions and open roads, the inhabitants of that March were much weakened and impoverished, so that they were no longer able to subsist without present help. The Queen and Council were informed thereof. To remedy this inconvenience they made choice of a worthy nobleman, my Lord Euers, to supply Sir John Foster's place; and, to enable him the better, he was allowed one hundred horsemen out of Yorkshire, to be disposed of at his pleasure, for the better quieting of the country. He came into his office with great joy and comfort for the poor inhabitants of the March, and to the terror and fear of the malefactors, expecting their utter ruin. But it oft falls out that seldom comes a better; for although his lordship did carefully employ his whole endeavour for the good of the March, and the destroying of malefactors, yet by trusting too much to men that he thought honest and faithful to him, he was deceived and abused for, for all his hundred horsemen, and his desire to have the country well governed, yet he had not long been there but the thieves were freed of their fear, and the poor inhabitants in worse case than ever. And to be short, the whole five years that he remained there, every year grew worse and worse; that none flourished but malefactors, who did what they listed, and harried and spoiled whole townships at their pleasure; so that the poor inhabitants were ready to fly their country, and to leave it waste. The Queen and Council were informed thereof, and my Lord himself made suit to leave his place, seeing himself abused by his officers whom he trusted, and could not tell how to help it.

Wardenship of the Middle March

About this time I had resigned my office of the East March to my Lord Willoughby, and was at court. Mr. Secretary sent for me to his chamber, and was desirous to know of me, whether I would accept it, if the Queen would confer on me the Warden of the Middle March. I said to him, I was a stranger to the country, and had a small acquaintance in it, and the March was much weakened and spoiled; yet, upon good conditions it might be I would accept it. He assured me that my demands should be very unreasonable if they were refused, and that I should be sure to have a hundred horse, as my Lord Euers had, and if I desired more he did not doubt but the Queen would grant them. I desired two days time to give my answer, which was granted. After I had conferred with my friends, and resolved what to do, I came to him and told him, that although I knew all things were out of order in the Middle March, and that the thieves did domineer, and do what they pleased, and that the poor inhabitants were utterly disabled and overthrown, yet was I not desirous to put the Queen and country to greater charge than was fitting; and whereas his lordship offered me more soldiers than my Lord Euers had, I did not desire so many; but if I might be allowed but forty horsemen, and they to be my own servants, and resident with me in my own house, I would put the Queen and country to no more charge, and would accept of the place. He was much amazed at my small demand, went presently to the Queen to acquaint her therewith. I had my demand granted, my commission with all speed signed, and I was sent down to execute my office.

I was no sooner come down but I removed my wife, children and household, to Alnwick Abbey, which was in the Middle March; the house where Sir John Foster ever lived when he was Warden. The first thing I did after I was settled in my office was to change my under officers. I made choice of Sir Henry Woodrington and Sir William Fenwick to be my two Deputy Wardens, and gave the one the keepership of Risdale the other that Liddesdale, and allowed them out of my forty horse, six apiece to attend them. I allowed Roger Woodrington two horsemen, who was employed by me on all occasions, and for the time I remained there did the Queen and country very great and good service. The rest of the horse I bestowed on my servants in my own house, which were gentlemen's sons in the country, and younger brothers of good rank; so that I had continually in my own stable (with my own provision) forty good horse, and good men able to ride them.

The thieves, hearing of my being settled there, continued still their wonted course in spoiling the country, not caring much for me nor my authority. It was the beginning of summer when I first entered into my office, but before that summer was ended they grew somewhat more fearful. For the first care I took was to clear the country of our inbred fears, the thieves within my March, for by them most mischief was done for the Scotch riders were always guided by some of them in all the spoils they made. God blessed me so well in all my designs as I never made a journey in vain, but did what I went for.

Amongst other malefactors there were two gentlemen thieves, that robbed and took purses from travellers in the highways (a theft that was never heard of in those parts before). I got them betrayed, took them, and sent them to Newcastle gaol, and there they were hanged.

I took not so few as sixteen or seventeen that summer, and the winter following, of notorious offenders, that ended their days by hanging or heading. When I was Warden of the East March, I had to do but with the opposite March which Sir Robert Kerr had; but here I had to do with the East, Middle, and West Marches of Scotland. I had very good justice with Sir Robert Kerr and the Laird of Fenhest, that had charge over the East part of the Middle March; but the West part, which was Liddesdale, and the West March, kept me a great while incumber. The first thing they did was the taking of Hartwesell, and carrying away of prisoners and all their goods. I sent to seek for justice for so great a wrong. The opposite officer sent me word, it was not in his power, for that they were all fugitives, and not answerable to the King's laws. I acquainted the King of

Scots with his answer. He signified to me that it was true, and that if I could take my own revenge without hurting his honest subjects, he would be glad of it. I took no long time to resolve what to do, but sent some two hundred horse to the place where the principal outliers lived, and took and brought away all the goods they had. The outlaws themselves were in strongholds, and could no way be got hold of. But one of the chief of them, being of more courage than the rest, got to horse and came pricking after them, crying out and asking, "What he was that durst avow that mighty work?" One of the company came to him with a spear and ran him through the body, leaving his spear broke in him, of which wound he died. The goods were divided to poor men from whom they were taken before.

This act so irritated the outlaws that they vowed cruel revenge, and that before the next winter was ended they would leave the whole country waste, that there should be none to resist them. His name was Sim of the Calfhill, that was killed (an Armstrong), and it was a Ridley of Hartwesell that killed him. They presently took a resolution to be revenged on that town. Thither they came, and set many houses of the town on fire, and took away all their goods; and as they were running up and down the streets with lights in their hands to set more houses on fire, there was one other of the Ridleys that was in a strong stone house that made a shot out amongst them, and it was his good hap to kill an Armstrong, one of the sons of the chiefest outlaw. The death of this young man wrought so deep an impression amongst them, as many vows were made that before the end of next winter they would lay the whole border waste. This [the murder] was done about the end of May. The chief of all these outlaws was old Sim of Whittram. He had five or six sons as able men as the borders had. This old man and his sons had not so few as two hundred at their commands, that were ever ready to ride with them to all actions at their beck.

The high parts of the March towards Scotland were put in a mighty fear, and the chief of them, for themselves and the rest, petitioned to me, and did assure me, that unless I did take some course with them by the end of that summer there was none of the inhabitants durst or would stay in their dwellings the next winter, but they would fly the country, and leave their houses and lands to the fury of the outlaws. Upon this complaint I called the gentlemen of the country together, and acquainted them with the misery that the highest parts of the March towards Scotland were likely to endure if there were not timely prevention to avoid it, and desired them to give me their best advice what course were fit to be taken. They all showed themselves willing to give me their best councils, and most of them were of opinion that I was not well advised to refuse the hundred horse that my Lord Euers had, and that now my best way was speedily to acquaint the Queen and Council with the necessity of having more soldiers, and that there could not be less than a hundred horse sent down for the defence of the country, besides the forty that I had already in pay, and that there was nothing but force of soldiers could keep them in awe; and to let the Council plainly understand, that the March of themselves were not able to subsist whenever the winter and long nights came in, unless present cure and remedy were provided for them.

I desired them to advise better of it, and to see if they could find out any other means to prevent their mischievous intentions without putting the Queen or country to any further charge. They all resolved there was no second means. Then I told them my intention what I meant to do, which was, "That myself with my two deputies, and the forty horse that I was allowed, would with what speed we could make ourselves ready to go up to the wastes, and there we would entrench ourselves, and lie as near as we could to the outlaws; and if there were any brave spirits among them that would go with us, they should be very welcome, and fare and lie as well as myself; and I did not doubt before the summer ended, to do something that should abate the pride of these outlaws." Those that were unwilling to hazard themselves liked not this motion. They said that in so doing I might keep the country in quiet the time I lay there, but when the winter approached I could stay there no longer, and that was the thieves' time to do all their mischief. But there were divers young gentlemen that offered to go with me, some with three, some with four horses, and to stay with me so long as I would there continue. I took a list of all those that offered to go with me, and found that with myself, my officers, the gentlemen and our servants, we should be about two hundred good men and horse: a competent number as I thought for such a service.

The day and place was appointed for our meeting in the wastes; and by the help of the foot of Liddesdale and Risdale, we had soon built a pretty fort, and within it we had all cabins made to lie in, and every one brought beds or mattresses to lie on. There we stayed from the middle of June till almost the end of August. We were between fifty and sixty gentlemen, besides their servants, and my horsemen so that we were not so few as two hundred horse. We wanted no provision for ourselves nor our horses; for the country people were well paid for anything they brought us, so that we had a good market every day before our fort, to buy what we lacked.

The chief outlaws at our coming fled their houses, where they dwelt, and betook themselves to a large and great forest (with all their goods), which was called the Tarras. It was of that strength, and so surrounded with bogs and marshy grounds, and thick bushes and shrubs, as they feared not the force nor power of England nor Scotland so long as they were there. They sent me word that I was like the first puff of a haggis, hottest at the first, and bade me stay there as long as the weather would give me leave; they would stay in the Tarras-wood, until I was weary of lying in the waste, and when I had had my time, and they no whit the worse, they would play their parts which should keep me waking the next winter. Those gentlemen of the country that came not with me were of the same mind, for they knew (or thought at least) that my force was not sufficient to withstand the fury of the outlaws. The time I stayed at the fort I was not idle, but cast by all means I could how to take them in the great strength they were in. I found a means to send a hundred and fifty horsemen into Scotland (conveyed by a muffled man not known to any of the company) thirty miles within Scotland, and the business was so carried that none in the country took any alarm at this passage.

They were quietly brought to the back side of the Tarras to Scotland-ward. There they divided themselves into three parts, and took up three passages which the outlaws made themselves secure of, if from England side they should at any time be put at. They had their scouts on the tops of hills on the English side, to give them warning if at any time any power of men should come to surprise them. The three ambushes were falsely laid without being discovered, and about four o'clock in the morning there were three hundred horse and a thousand foot that came directly to the place where the scouts lay. They gave the alarum our men broke down as fast as they could into the wood. The outlaws thought themselves safe, assuring themselves at any time to escape; but they were so strongly set upon on the English side as they were forced to leave their goods and to betake themselves to their passages towards Scotland. There were presently five taken of the principal of them. The rest, seeing themselves (as they thought) betrayed, retired into the thick woods and bogs, that our men durst not follow them, for fear of losing themselves. The principal of the five that were taken were two of the eldest sons of Sim of Whitram. These five they brought to me to the fort, and a number of goods both of sheep and kine, which satisfied most part of the country that they had stolen them from.

The five that were taken were of great worth and value amongst them, insomuch that for their liberty I should have what conditions I should demand or desire. First, all English prisoners were set at liberty. Then had I themselves and most part of the gentlemen of the Scottish side so strictly bound in bonds, to enter to me, in fifteen days warning, any offender, that they durst not for their lives break any covenant that I made with them and so upon these conditions I set them at liberty, and was never after troubled with these kind of people. Thus God blessed me in bringing this great trouble to so quiet an end, we broke up our fort, and every man retired to his own house.

After God had put an end to this troublesome business, I rested in quiet the rest of the summer, and the next winter after; and had leisure by little and little to purge the Marsh of inbred thieves, and God so blessed me that I failed not in any of my undertakings, but did effect what I went for, which did so astonish all the malefactors as they were afraid to offend; so that the Marsh rested very quiet from the invasion of the foreign, and from the petty stealths of the thieves that lived amongst ourselves.

The next summer after I fell into a cumbersome trouble, but it was not in the nature of thieves or malefactors. There had been an ancient custom of the borderers when they were at quiet, for the opposite border to send to the Warden of the Middle Marsh, to desire leave that they might come into the borders of England, and hunt with their greyhounds for deer, towards the end of summer, which was never denied them. But towards the end of Sir John Foster's government, when he grew very old and weak, they took boldness upon them, and without leave asking would come into England, and hunt at their pleasure, and stay their own time; and when they were a hunting, their servants would come with carts and cut down as much wood as every one thought would serve his turn, and carry it away to their houses in Scotland. Sir John's imbecility and weakness occasioned them to continue this misdemeanour some four or five years together, before he left his office. And after my Lord Euers had the office, he was so vexed and troubled with the disorders of the country, as all the time he remained there he had no leisure to think of so small a business, and to redress it; so that now they began to hold it lawful to come and go at their pleasures without leave asking. The first summer I entered they did the like. The Armstrongs kept me so on work that I had no time to redress it. But having over-mastered them, and the whole Marsh being brought to a good stay and quietness, the beginning of next summer I wrote to Ferniherst, the Warden over against me, to desire him to acquaint the gentlemen of March, that I was no way unwilling to hinder them of their accustomed sports to hunt in England as they ever had done, but withal I would not by my default dishonour the Queen and myself to give them more liberty than was fitting: I prayed him therefore to let them know, that if they would, according to the ancient custom, send to me for leave, they should have all the contentment I could give them if otherwise they would continue their wonted course, I would do my best to hinder them.

Notwithstanding this letter, within a month after they came and hunted as they used to do without leave, and cut down wood and carried it away. I wrote again to the Warden, and plainly told him I would not suffer one other affront, but if they came again without leave, they should dearly aby it. For all this they would not be warned, but towards the end of the summer they came again to their wonted sports. I had taken order to have present word brought me, which was done. I sent my two deputies with all the speed they could make, and they took along with them such gentlemen as were in their way, with my forty horse, and about one of the clock they came to them and set upon them; some hurt was done, but I gave especial order they should do as little hurt and shed as little blood as possibly they could. They observed my command, only they broke all their carts, and took a dozen of the principal gentlemen that were there, and brought them to me to Witherington, where I then lay. I made them welcome, and gave them the best entertainment that I could. They lay in the castle two or three days, and so I sent them home; they assuring me that they would never hunt there again without leave, which they did truly perform all the time I stayed there; and I many times met them myself, and hunted with them two or three days; and so we continued good neighbours ever after. But the King complained to the Queen very grievously of this fact. The Queen and Council liked very well of what I had done; but to give the King some satisfaction to content him, my two officers were commanded to the Bishop of Durham's, there to remain prisoners during her Majesty's pleasure. Within a fortnight I had them out again, and there was no more of this business. The rest of the time I stayed there it was governed with great quietness.

In this state was this Middle March when King James came in King of England; and in all the time I continued officer there, God so blessed me, and all the actions I took in hand, that I never failed of any one enterprise, but they were all effected to my own desire, and the good of that government. Thus passed I forty-two of my years, God assisting me with his blessing and mighty protection.

The Death of Queen Elizabeth and the Ride to Edinburgh

After that all things were quieted, and the border in safety, towards the end of five years that I had been Warden there, having little to do I resolved upon a journey to court, to see my friends and renew my acquaintance there. I took my journey about the end of the year. When I came to court I found the Queen ill disposed, and she kept her inner lodging; yet she, hearing of my arrival, sent for me. I found her in one of her withdrawing chambers, sitting low upon her cushions. She called me to her, I kissed her hand, and told her it was my chiefest happiness to see her in safety and in health, which I wished might long continue. She took me by the hand, and wrung it hard, and said, "No, Robin, I am not well," and then discoursed with me of her indisposition, and that her heart had been sad and heavy for ten or twelve days, and in her discourse she fetched not so few as forty or fifty great sighs. I was grieved at the first to see her in this plight; for in all my lifetime before I never knew her fetch a sigh, but when the Queen of Scots was beheaded. Then upon my knowledge she shed many tears and sighs, manifesting her innocence that she never gave consent to the death of that Queen.

I used the best words I could to persuade her from this melancholy humour; but I found by her it was too deep rooted in her heart, and hardly to be removed. This was upon a Saturday night, and she gave command that the great closet should be prepared for her to go to chapel the next morning. The next day, all things being in a readiness, we long expected her coming. After eleven o'clock, one of the grooms came out and bade make ready for the private closet, she would not go to the great. There we stayed long for her coming, but at the last she had cushions laid for her in the privy chamber hard by the closet door, and there she heard service.

From that day forwards she grew worse and worse. She remained upon her cushions four days and nights at the least.

All about her could not persuade her either to take any sustenance or go to bed.

I, hearing that neither the physicians nor none about her could persuade her to take any course for her safety, feared her death would soon after ensue. I could not but think in what a wretched estate I should be left, most of my livelihood depending on her life. And hereupon I bethought myself with what grace and favour I was ever received by the King of Scots, whensoever I was sent to him. I did assure myself it was neither unjust nor unhonest for me to do for myself, if God at that time should call her to his mercy. Hereupon I wrote to the King of Scots (knowing him to be the right heir to the crown of England) and certified him in what state her Majesty was. I desired him not to stir from Edinburgh; if of that sickness she should die, I would be the first man that should bring him news of it.

The Queen grew worse and worse, because she would be so, none about her being able to persuade her to go to bed. My Lord Admiral was sent for (who by reason of my sister's death, that was his wife, had absented himself some fortnight from court) what by fair means, what by force, he got her to bed. There was no hope of her recovery, because she refused all remedies.

On Wednesday, the twenty-third of March, she grew speechless. That afternoon, by signs, she called for her Council, and by putting her hand to her head, when the King of Scots was named to succeed her, they all knew he was the man she desired should reign after her.

About six at night she made signs for the Archbishop and her Chaplains to come to her, at which time I went in with them, and sat upon my knees full of tears to see that heavy sight. Her Majesty lay upon her back, with one hand in the bed, and the other without. The Bishop kneeled down by her, and examined her first of her faith, and she so punctually answered all his several questions, by lifting up her eyes and holding up her hand, as it was a comfort to all the beholders. Then the good man told her plainly what she was, and what she was to come to; and though she had been long a great Queen here upon earth, yet shortly she was to yield an account of her stewardship to the King of Kings. After this he began to pray, and all that were by did answer him. After he had continued long in prayer, till the old man's knees were weary, he blessed her, and meant to rise and leave her. The Queen made a sign with her hand. My sister Scrope, knowing her meaning, told the Bishop the Queen desired he would pray still. He did so for a long half-hour after, and then thought to leave her. The second time she made sign to have him continue in prayer. He did so for half an hour more, with earnest cries to God for her soul's health, which he uttered with that fervency of spirit as the Queen to all our sight much rejoiced thereat, and gave testimony to us all of her Christian and comfortable end. By this time it grew late, and every one departed, all but her women that attended her.

This that I heard with my ears, and did see with my eyes, I thought it my duty to set down, and to affirm it for a truth, upon the faith of a Christian, because I know there have been many false lies reported of the end and death of that good lady.

I went to my lodging, and left word with one in the Cofferer's chamber to call me, if that night it was thought she would die, and gave the porter an angel to let me in at any time when I called. Between one and two of the clock on Thursday morning, he that I left in the Cofferer's chamber brought me word the Queen was dead. I rose and made all the haste to the gate to get in. There I was answered, I could not enter; the Lords of the Council having been with him, and commanded him that none should go in or out, but by warrant from them. At the very instant, one of the Council (the Comptroller) asked whether I was at the gate. I said yes. He said to me, if I pleased he would let me in. I desired to know how the Queen did. He answered, "Pretty well." I bade him good night. He replied, and said, "Sir, if you will come in, I will give you my word and credit you shall go out again at your own pleasure." Upon his word I entered the gate, and came up to the Cofferer's chamber, where I found all the ladies weeping bitterly. He led me from thence to the privy chamber, where all the Council was assembled; there I was caught hold of, and assured I should not go for Scotland, till their pleasures were farther known. I told them I came of purpose to that end. From thence they all went to the Secretary's chamber, and as they went they gave a special command to the porters that none should go out of the gates but such servants as they should send to prepare their coaches and horses for London. There was I left in the midst of the court to think my own thoughts till they had done counsel.

I went to my brother's chamber, who was in bed, having been over-watched many nights before. I got him up with all speed, and when the Council's men were going out of the gate, my brother thrust to the gate. The porter knowing him to be a great officer, let him out. I pressed after him, and was stayed by the porter. My brother said angrily to the porter, "Let him out, I will answer for him." Whereupon I was suffered to pass, which I was not a little glad of.

I got to horse, and rode to the Knight Marshal's lodging by Charing Cross, and there stayed till the Lords came to Whitehall Garden. I stayed there till it was nine o'clock in the morning, and hearing that all the Lords were in the old orchard at Whitehall, I sent the Marshal to tell them that I had stayed all that while to know their pleasures, and that I would attend them if they would command me any service. They were very glad when they heard I was not gone, and desired the Marshal to send for me, and I should with all speed be despatched for Scotland.

The Marshal believed them, and sent Sir Arthur Savage for me. I made haste to them. One of the Council (my Lord of Banbury that now is) whispered the Marshal in the ear, and told him, if I came they would stay me, and send some other in my stead. The Marshal got from them, and met me coming to them between the two gates. He bade me be gone, for he had learned for certain that if I came to them they would betray me.

I returned and took horse between nine and ten o'clock, and that night rode to Doncaster. The Friday night I came to my own house at Witherington, and presently took order with my deputies to see the borders kept in quiet, which they had much to do: and gave order the next morning the King of Scotland should be proclaimed King of England, and at Morpeth and Alnwick. Very early on Saturday I took horse for Edinburgh, and came to Norham about twelve at noon, so that I might well have been with the King at supper time: but I got a great fall by the way, and my horse with one of his heels gave me a great blow on the head that made me shed much blood. It made me so weak that I was forced to ride a soft pace after, so that the King was newly gone to bed by the time that I knocked at the gate.

I was quickly let in, and carried up to the King's chamber. I kneeled by him, and saluted him by his title of England, Scotland, France and Ireland. He gave me his hand to kiss, and bade me welcome. After he had long discoursed of the manner of the Queen's sickness and of her death, he asked what letters I had from the Council? I told him, none: and acquainted him how narrowly I escaped from them. And yet I had brought him a blue ring from a fair lady, that I hoped would give him assurance of the truth that I had reported. He took it and looked upon it, and said, "It is enough: I know by this you are a true messenger." Then he committed me to the charge of my Lord Home, and gave straight command that I should want nothing. He sent for his chirurgeons to attend me, and when I kissed his hand at my departure he said to me these gracious words: "I know you have lost a near kinswoman, and a loving mistress; but take here my hand, I will be as good a master to you, and will requite this service with honour and reward."

So I left him that night, and went with my Lord Hume to my lodging, where I had all things fitting for so weary a man as I was. After my head was dressed, I took leave of my Lord and many others that attended me, and went to my rest.

The next morning by ten o'clock my Lord Hume was sent to me from the King, to know how I had rested; and withal said, that his Majesty commanded him to know of me what it was that I desired most, that he should do for me; bade me ask, and it should be granted. I desired my Lord to say to his Majesty from me, that I had no reason to importune him for any suit, for that I had not as yet done him any service: but my humble request to his Majesty was, to admit me a gentleman of his bedchamber, and hereafter, I knew, if his Majesty saw me worthy, I should not want to taste of his bounty. My Lord returned this answer, that he sent me word back, "with all his heart, I should have my request." And the next time I came to court (which was some four days after) at night, I was called into his bedchamber, and there by my Lord of Richmond, in his presence, I was sworn one of the gentlemen of his bedchamber, and presently I helped to take off his clothes, and stayed till he was in bed. After this there came daily gentlemen and noblemen from our court, and the King set down a fixed day for his departure towards London.

Upon the report of the Queen's death the East border broke forth into great unruliness, insomuch as many complaints came to the King thereof. I was desirous to go to appease them, but I was so weak and ill of my head that I was not able to undertake such a journey, but I offered that I would send my two deputies that should appease the trouble and make them quiet, which was by them shortly after effected.

In the Court of King James

Now was I to begin a new world; for by the King's coming to the crown I was to lose the best part of my living. For my office of Wardenry ceased, and I lost the pay of forty horse, which were not so little (both) as a thousand pounds per annum. Most of the great ones in court envied my happiness when they heard I was sworn of the King's bedchamber: and in Scotland I had no acquaintance. I only relied on God and the King. The one never left me, the other shortly after his coming to London deceived my expectation, and adhered to those that sought my ruin.

At the King's coming to the Tower there was, at the least, twenty Scotch gentlemen discharged of the bedchamber, and sworn gentlemen of the privy chamber, amongst which (some that wished me little good had such credit with the King that) I was to go the same way that the rest did; out of God's blessing into the warm sun. I could not help it. Those that ruled the helm had so resolved it; and I was forced to that I could not help. All the comfort that I had was the King's assurance that I should shortly be admitted to his bedchamber again. And whereas I was promised one hundred pounds per annum in fee farm, it was cut short to one hundred marks. Thus all things went cross with me, and patience was my best companion. He that did me most hurt, and was greedy of Naboth's vineyard, gave me that counsel which I followed, and I found after it did me much good. He told me he knew the King better than I did, and assured me that if the King did perceive in me a discontented mind, I should never have his love nor favour again. I had a sad heart, yet still before the King I showed myself merry and jovial.

This continued until the Queen came up, which was the next summer. My wife waited on her; and at Windsor was sworn of her privy chamber, and mistress of her sweet coffers, and had a lodging allowed her in court. This was some comfort to me, that I had my wife so near me. Shortly after her coming she made suit for James Hayes to be admitted again into the bedchamber with Philip Herbert. I bestirred myself as well as I could, and charged the King with his promise, but could do no good. They were taken in, and poor I refused, never after to hope for it.

They left me not thus that wished me evil, but having nothing but Norham to live on, my good Lord of Dunbar begged the keeping of it over my head, and I did see it was folly to strive, and therefore thought on the next best course to do myself good. Dunbar thirsted after nothing more than to get of me the possession of Norham. My Lord Cecil was umpire between us: he offered five thousand pounds: I held it at seven thousand: six thousand pounds was agreed upon, which was truly paid, and did me more good than if I had kept Norham. After the agreement made, having received two thousand pounds, the rest I was to have at three months and three months, I then took my journey to the North to give his agents possession of Norham. I sold them there as much goods as, when I returned back, I received of my Lord Dunbar eight hundred pounds for.

When I was at Norham, God put it into my mind to go to Dunfermline, to see the King's second son. I found him a very weak child. I stayed a day or two with my Lord of Dunfermline, whom I had long known, and was my noble friend, and so returned to court again.

The summer after my Lord Dunfermline and his Lady were to bring up the young Duke. The King was at Theobalds, when he heard that they were past Northumberland; from thence the King sent me to meet them, and gave me commission to see them furnished with all things necessary, and to stay with them till they had brought the Duke to court. I did so, and found the Duke at Bishop Auckland. I attended his Grace all his journey up, and at Sir George Farmer's in Northamptonshire we found the King and Queen, who were very glad to see their young son.

There were many great ladies suitors for the keeping of the Duke; but when they did see how weak a child he was, and not likely to live, their hearts were down, and none of them was desirous to take charge of him.

After my Lord Chancellor of Scotland and his Lady had stayed here from Midsummer till towards Michaelmas, they were to return for Scotland and to leave the Duke behind them. The Queen (by approbation of the Lord Chancellor) made choice of my wife to have the care and keeping of the Duke. Those who wished me no good were glad of it, thinking that if the Duke should die in our charge (his weakness being such as gave them great cause to suspect it) then it would not be thought fit that we should remain in court after. My gracious God left me not, but out of weakness he showed his strength, and beyond all men's expectations so blessed the Duke with health and strength, under my wife's charge, as he grew better and better every day. The King and Queen rejoiced much to see him prosper as he did, and my wife for the care she had of him and her diligence (which indeed was great) was well esteemed of them both, as did well appear. For by her procurement when I was from court she got me a suit of the King that was worth to me afterwards four or five thousand pounds. I had the charge given me of the Duke's household, and none allowed to his service but such as I gave way to, by which means I preferred to him a number of my own servants. In the meantime that my wife had the charge of him, my daughter was brought up with the King's daughter and served her, and had the happiness to be allowed to wait on her in the privy lodgings. My wife and self, by waiting still in the privy lodgings of the Duke, got better esteem of the King and Queen.

The Duke was past four years old when he was first delivered to my wife; he was not able to go, nor scant stand alone, he was so weak in his joints, and especially his ankles, insomuch as many feared they were out of joint. Yet God so blessed him both with health and strength that he proved daily stronger and stronger. Many a battle my wife had with the King, but she still prevailed. The King was desirous that the string under his tongue should be cut, for he was so long beginning to speak as he thought he would never have spoke. Then he would have him put in iron boots, to strengthen his sinews and joints; but my wife protested so much against them both as she got the victory, and the King was fain to yield. My wife had the charge of him from a little past four, till he was almost eleven years old in all which time he daily grew more and more in health and strength both of body and mind, to the amazement of many that knew his weakness when she first took charge of him. Now was my wife to leave her charge, and the Duke to have none but men to attend upon him. My wife had four hundred pounds a year pension during her life, and admitted to the Queen's service in the place she was before, and so with great grief took leave of her dear master the Duke.

And now began anew more troubles for me to run through; for it was resolved by some of my ill-wishers that I should leave his service when my wife went from him. And to that end there was a Scotch gentleman of great learning, and very good worth, sent for out of Ireland from his service there, to be placed as chief governor over the Duke, both in his bedchamber, and over his household; and Prince Henry the chief instrument of his preferment. Over he came, and daily expected to receive his charge by the appointment of the King and Council: and to that end a Council was called, the King being present, where it was propounded that this gentleman should be chief gentleman of his bed-chamber, master of his robes, and commander of his household and family: and for that I had served him long, they would not clean dismiss me, but I should be of his bedchamber still, and keeper of his privy purse. It was near concluding that it should be so, but my God, that never forsook me, put it into the mind of my Lord Chamberlain Suffolk to say something for me. It was no more but this; he said to the King, "Sir, this gentleman that is recommended to be so near the Duke, I have heard much worth of him, and by report he is a fit man for near attendance about his Grace. Notwithstanding, give me leave, I beseech you, to speak my knowledge of my cousin Carey. I have known him long, and the manner of his living. There was none in the late Queen's court that lived in a better fashion than he did. He so behaved himself that he was beloved of all in court and elsewhere; wheresoever he went the company he kept was of the best, as well noblemen as others. He carried himself so as every honest man was glad of his company. He ever spent with the best, and wore as good clothes as any, and he exceeded in making choice of what he wore to be handsome and comely. His birth I need speak nothing of: it is known well enough. I leave him to your Majesty to dispose of: only this, sure I am, there is none about the Duke that knows how to furnish him with clothes and apparel so well as he; and therefore in my opinion he is the fittest man to be master of the robes."

This cast the scales. The King took hold of his speech, and said he had spoken justly and honestly; my birth and breeding requiring the chief place about his son, and I should have it, and the mastership of his robes; he should do me a great deal of wrong else. Hereupon, though many were mad against it, yet the King's pleasure being signified, there durst none oppose, but it was by the Council concluded that I should be sworn chief gentleman of his bedchamber, and of the office of his robes; and the other of his bedchamber, and master of his privy purse. The King and Council being risen, word was with all speed sent to St. James's to Prince Henry of what was decreed. By the persuasion of some about him he came to Whitehall in all haste to alter this resolution. He was much discontented, and greatly desired an alteration. The King sent for my Lord Chamberlain. The Prince was very earnest, and something angry at my Lord that he had said so much. He very nobly excused himself; that he had said no more but what he knew to be true. After long dispute, and that the Prince saw the King was unwilling to alter what was resolved by the Council, he said to my Lord, "I hope it shall not offend you, if I can get Sir Robert Carey himself to accept of the 'second place.'" He answered, no: what I consented to should satisfy him; so they parted, and the Prince came to St. James's much troubled. I had word what passed betwixt them. To St. James's I went, and attended in the Prince's privy chamber to know his pleasure, looking still when he should call to speak with me. I stayed two days, and heard no word from him. The third after supper, he called me to the cupboard, and thus began: "You know my brother is to have his household settled, and there are two places about him of equal worth; and because you have served him long, and are nobly born, it is reason you should have your choice. There is the surveyorship of his lands (which I take to be the best place) and the mastership of his robes. You have many friends, and by having that office you may do them and yourself good. The other I take to be a place of no such import. I thought good to know of yourself which you would make choice of." I humbly thanked him, that he gave me that respect in advising me to that which he thought best; but I humbly craved pardon, alleging my insufficiency in the one, which, if I should accept, I should wrong my master and discredit myself; and if I had skill in anything, I thought I could tell how to make good clothes; and therefore desired humbly I might continue in the place I had; and that he would please to dispose of the other as he liked. He was satisfied with my answer, and within two days after I was sworn chief gentleman of the bedchamber, and master of the robes; and the other, gentleman of the bedchamber, master of the privy purse, and surveyor-general of his lands.

This storm was thus blown over, and I was settled as I desired. I continued so a long time, and God so blessed me as I had the favour and good opinion of the King, and regained my credit with that worthy Prince, that, maugre the malice of some near about him, he thought me honest and faithful to the King, himself and his brother: and daily more and more I found the Prince to conceive better and better of me. But the hopes I had of him did quickly vanish, for within two years after, it pleased God to call to his mercy that hopeful and brave Prince, *that was a terror to his enemies, and a sure anchor to his friends;* and that small time he lived here he employed it so worthily as the loss of him was so grievous to all the subjects of this island that no expression of sorrow could enough manifest their grief.

The Duke by succession was then Prince; and before I could imagine any mischief to be plotted against me, there was a sure groundwork laid (as they thought) to supplant me, and put me from being his Chamberlain at his creation when he was Prince of Wales. Long before the time, one near about the Prince would often say to me that at his creation I was sure to be his Chamberlain; but then I could not be of his bedchamber. I did always answer, that I would not be put out of his bedchamber for any other office that could be given me; but I did see no reason why I should not hold them both. This kind of language he held oft with me. At last before the Prince in his school-chamber, he began the like speech, the Prince affirming I could not be both. I then suspected something, and pleaded for myself that there was a present example of my Lord of Somerset, who was the King's Chamberlain, and yet kept the bedchamber. It was alleged that he was a favourite, but never any before had them both. I said there was as great reason for me to be Chamberlain and of his bedchamber as for another to be his Surveyor-General, and to hold his place in the bed-chamber. That was said to be but a petty office, but the Chamberlain's place was of a high nature. This discourse was moved before the Prince, of purpose that he might hear me refuse the Chamberlain's place, except I might continue my place in the bedchamber (which was all they desired). Shortly after they got the Prince to confirm to the King what he heard me say, that I would not be his Chamberlain, to lose my place in the bedchamber. Then they pleaded to the King how unfit it was that any man should hold both places; and that there was no example that ever Prince had the like: insomuch as they brought the King to their opinion. Then the King was wrought on to make my Lord of Roxborough the Prince's Chamberlain, which was concluded; but kept so secret as none knew of it but the King, the Prince, my good friend, and Roxborough. This was about Easter. On a sudden it was resolved that the Prince should, the midsummer after, be created some ten days before the time it was whispered that Roxborough should be Chamberlain, and at last it came to my ears. The court was fully persuaded that none but myself should hold the place, which made me think it would be a great disgrace to me to miss it, and made me use the best means I could to get the place, and prevent them. After I got the true knowledge of all their proceedings, and how the King and Prince were brought in by a wile to give the place from me, I addressed myself to the Queen, told her all I knew, and how secretly it had been plotted and wrought. I humbly besought her Majesty to interpose for me. When she heard me, she could not believe that Roxborough, or his friend, durst or would seek so eminent a place under her son without her knowledge and consent. But when by Roxborough's wife she was assured of it, she sent for me again, and told me it was true that I had said, but bade me trouble myself no further: her wrong was more than mine, and she would right both herself and me. Presently she made known both to Roxborough and his friend in what disdain she took it, that they durst undertake such a business without acquainting her, and vowed they should buy the neglect of her at a dear rate. She kept her word; for Roxborough was presently sent into Scotland in her high disgrace, and never after saw her; my other friend felt her heavy hand a long time after. And at the Prince's creation, which was the Michaelmas following, I was sworn the Prince's Chamberlain, and continued of his bedchamber. Thus did God raise up the Queen to take my part, and by her means the storm that was so strongly plotted against me was brought to nought.

Then was the Prince's house settled; and amongst other officers, Sir John Villiers was sworn of his bedchamber, and Sir Robert Kerr; the one made master of the robes, the other keeper of the privy purse; Sir James Fullerton, groom of the stole, and Mr. Murray, secretary.

Long before this had I married my daughter to Lord Wharton's son and heir. My eldest son was, at the Prince's creation, made a Knight of the Bath (who was then newly come from travel), and, by the Queen's means, my youngest son was, before his creation, sworn a groom of his bedchamber. My wife waited on the Queen, and myself on the Prince; so (for the time it lasted) we lived at no great charge, and most of the little means we had we employed as it came in to the bettering of our estate.

But it continued not long thus, for within four years after, or thereabouts, the Queen died; her house dissolved, and my wife was forced to keep house and family, which was out of our way a thousand pounds a year that we saved before. In this state I continued until I came to the age of almost sixty years, in favour both with the King and my master. About this time I married my eldest son to the eldest daughter of Sir Lionel Cranfield, afterwards Earl of Middlesex, and Lord Treasurer of England. Not long after, by my master's means, the King made me Baron of Leppington. Two years after, the Prince and my Lord of Buckingham went from Theobalds to New-hall. The 17th of February the King went to Newmarket. There the Prince appointed myself and the rest of his servants to meet him two days after. But the first news that we heard was that the Prince

and my Lord Duke were gone for Spain. This made a great
hubbub in our court, and in all England besides. I was
appointed to go after him by sea, and to carry such servants of
his with me as the Prince had left word should come after, and
such others as the King allowed. I had a large commission made
me for the government, and to keep in good order those that
went with me. From Portsmouth we set sail about the middle of
March, and the fourth day after we landed at St. Andero's in
Biscay, and there I received a letter from the Prince, that all his
servants should return back in the ship they came, only myself
and my Lord Compton should come to him to Madrid. To Madrid
I came some six days after; before which time the Prince had
remanded his servants to come to him. There I stayed some
month with the Prince, by which time he found that his stay
there would be longer than he expected. He considered my
years, and feared the heat of the year coming fast on would
much distemper me, and therefore persuaded me to return for
England, and sent a great many of his servants back with me.
We returned in the ship we came, and landed at Portland in
Dorsetshire. There I took post, and came to Greenwich to the
King. I delivered him the Prince's letters, and after some
discourse had with me, I kissed his hand, took my leave of him,
and came to my own house, where I remained very privately
until the Prince's return. I must not forget God's goodness
towards me in this journey. I was then upon sixty-three years of
age (years not well agreeing with such a journey), but God so
blessed me from the first to the last, as I continued in perfect
health and all the time I was in Spain I had such a stomach to
my meat as in my younger days I never had the like.

At Michaelmas after, to the comfort of all true English hearts,
the Prince landed at Portsmouth. After this, the match was
broken off with Spain, and a treaty in France for the King's
youngest sister. My Lord of Holland was employed Ambassador
for this service, and my Lord of Carlisle sent after him for
assistance. Many tos and fros there were before it was
concluded. Two years or more were spent in this affair, and
when it was come to a full point of agreement on all parts, the
King fell sick of a tertian ague at Theobalds, and, to the grief of

all true hearts, died of that sickness the 27th day of March, in the twenty-second year of his reign.

And now began afresh, in my old years, new troubles: for whereas heretofore all Princes, when they came to be Kings, had an especial care to prefer their old servants, or at least to let them hold the places they had under them whilst they were Princes; it fell out otherwise with us. For myself being his Chamberlain, and the rest (as the Master of the horse, Treasurer, Comptroller, and Secretary) were all discharged of our places; and those that served in those offices in the old King's time, continued in them still. But the King dealt very graciously with us, and for the loss of our places, gave the most of us good rewards. To myself in particular, he gave (to me and my heirs for ever) five hundred per annum in fee farm, which was a very bountiful gift, and a good satisfaction for the loss of my office and especially because I continued my place of gentleman of the bedchamber.

In May after, the King went to Dover to meet his new Queen, and by the time he came back with her to Whitehall, the plague grew so hot in London, as none that could tell how to get out of it, would stay there. The King and Queen removed to Hampton Court. The infection grew hotter and hotter. The Parliament was removed to Oxford. The plague grew hot there too, so that what for that and other discontents, the Parliament was dissolved. The King went in progress to Beauly. The Queen returned to Oatlands and Nonsuch, and I and my family to Kenilworth, where we stayed the summer. Towards Michaelmas the plague began to decrease. The King returning from his progress, was met by the Queen at Salisbury, at which place I found his Majesty (leaving my wife and family at Kenilworth). I waited on him until he returned southward, and [also waited on him] at Windsor.

Some ten days before Christmas the King and Queen went to keep their Christmas at Hampton Court, and I returned to Kenilworth, and stayed there ten days after Christmas, where I heard of a new Parliament to begin the 8th of February, and that the King was to be crowned at Westminster, the 6th thereof. I returned to court, and among others that the King pleased to give honours to at his coronation, I was created Earl of Monmouth.

APPENDICES

Appendix 1

Robert Carey's Letters

The following letters are reproduced *verbatim* froim the 1905 edition, complete with the wonders of 16th Century spelling.

Sir Robert Carey to the Lord Hunsdon, his father

May it please your Lordship t' understande, that yesterday yn the afternoone, I stoode by her Majestic, as she was att cards yn the presens chamber. She cawide me too her, and asket me, when you ment too go too Barwyke? I towide hyr, that you determynde to begyn your journey presently after Whytsontyd. She grew yntoo a grate rage, begynnynge with Gods Wonds, that she wolde sett you by the feete; and sende another yn your place, if you dalyed with her thus ; for she wolde nott be thus dalyed with all. I towlde her, that with as much possyble speed as myght be, you wolde departe; and that your lying att London thys fortnyght was too no other ende but to make provysion for your jorney. She anseryd me, that you have byn goynge from Crystmas too Ester, and from Ester to Whytsonday; but if you differde the tyme any longer, she wolde appoynt some uther yn your place; and thys message she commandyd me to send you.

Your Lps humble and obedycnt Sunne,
R.   CAREY.

To the Ryghte Honorable my very goode L. and Father, my L. of Hunsden.

Henry Lord Hunsdon to Lord Burghley, Treasurer of England

My very goode Lord,

Havynge alwayse founde your L. my goode L. and frende more then any uther, I am the bowlder too acquaynte your L. with a harde accydente too me, such as I thynke your L. wolde sa hardly beleve, as I dyd lyttell looke for ytt.
Thys day at dyner I recevyd a letter from my sunn Robartt Carey, of such speechys as hyr Majestie eusy'd unto hym upon Sunday towchynge me; which for brevyty sake I sende your L. the coppy of; wheryn I thynk my self so hardly delte with all by her Majestie, as I cannott beyre it, nor obay itt yn suche sort, as she commands ytt.

My L. I have never refusyd to serve hyr; howsoever she commandyd me, so longe as I was able; and beynge now, by reason of the maryagys of my two dawters, and besyds theyr maryage-mony, was att as grete chargys with the tyme of theyr maryagys, as theyr maryage-mony came unto; beynge now commanded too repayre to Barwyke, I desyerde only att hyr Majestic's hands the lone of £1000 too be payde upon my intertaynment of Barwyke and the wardenery, wherof too be repayde the one halfe at Mychalmas next, and the uther halfe at our Lady day, whyche to be borrowyde of a marchant, the interest comes nott too 100 £. and trewly I wolde nott have made so symple a scute unto hyr, but thatt apon thes occasyons aforesayde I hade layde all my platte to gage, without which I cowlde nott with any credytt go thyther; and hopynge, that she would consyder so farr of my nede, I have stayde herapon, the rather knowynge the matters both of Scottland and the Bordars too be yn suche state, as ther was no suche necessityc of my said hasty goynge to Barwike. But syns I fynde her Majestic so small care of my necessyte, and so redy to threten mee, not only with the placynge of summe uther yn my place, butt also too impryson me; syns my suytt ys no better consyderyd of by

85

hyr, and that her Majestic ys so reddy apon so small cawse too deale thus (nott hardly) but extremely with me, as I hade the offyce of Barwyke of her Majestie specyally, and only by your L. goode meanes agenste the wylls of uthers, who sought too putt me by ytt, too preferre uthers of theyr frends unto ytt so am I most hartely too pray your L. that as you were the only brynger of me too that office, wheryn I hope I have performyd my dewty, bothe for her Majestic's servys, and for the goode of the hole countrey, bothe too her Majestie's honor, the benyfitt of the cuntrey, the commendacyon of your L, who preferde me unto yet, and too myne owne credytt, yn despight of myn ennymys whersoever; so I humbly pray your L. thatt syns I see, that hyr Majestie ys so reddy to place sume uther yn ytt, that your L. wyl be a meanes, that I may with her favor departe withal!, as I dyd with hyr goode favour receive ytt for an offyce of that charge ys not to be govern'd by any, that hath no better credytt or countenance of hyr Majcstie's then I have; for I am nott ignorent, what qwarrels may bc pykt too any mane, that hathe such a charge, if the Prynce shall be reddy, nott only too heare every complaynte, whyther ytt be false or trew and so apon imagynacion too, condemn without cause. Well! my L. Gode sende them joy, that shall succede me ; and too do her Majestic no worse servys theryn, then I have done; assurynge your L. that I will parte from ytt with a better wyll (fyndyng my selfe yn no better grace with hyr Majestic than I do) then ever I was too receive ytt. I am the bowldcr too trouble your L. thys muchc, because I doo by thys bearer wryght lyttle les to hyr Majestic: and for any imprysonment she cane use too me, ytt shall redownde too hyr dyshonor, because I neyther have nor wyll deserve ytt, and therfore ytt shall nott troble me.

Thus havynge byn over tedyous too your L. I commytt your L. too the tuycion of th' almyghty.

At Hunsdon this 8 of June 1584.

Your L. to command;
Hunsdon.

To the Ryght Honorable, and my very goode L.
 my L. Burghley, L. Hyghe Tresurar of England.

Appendix 2

Links

The following are good sources of information about the Borders Reivers and the turbulent times in which Robert Carey lived:

http://www.theborderers.info/index.html

www.sorbie.net/border_reivers.htm

http://www.electricscotland.com/history/other/border_reivers1.htm

http://www.nwlink.com/~scotlass/border.htm

Ripping Yarns.com's website is at:

www.RippingYarns.com

Appendix 3

Other Suggested Reading

The following list of books is not exhaustive, but will be of interest to those who want to find out more about the Border Reivers.

The following book is the definitive book on the history of the Border Reivers and is highly recommended:
"The Steel Bonnets" George MacDonald Fraser.
HarperCollins. ISBN 0002727463.

The following book is lavishly illustrated, although it covers the history in less detail than "The Steel Bonnets".
"The Border Reivers", Keith Durham, Angus McBride.
Osprey Books, ISBN 1855324172.

P.F. Chisholm has written a series of fiction books, with Robert Carey as the main character. These are worth looking out for if you are interested in the "atmosphere" of the times. The books are:
"A Famine of Horses"
"A Season of Knives"
"A Surfeit of Guns"
"A Plague of Angels"

Appendix 4

Other Books from Ripping Yarns.com

Ripping Yarns.com publishes a range of classic adventure books. Some of our titles include:

"Escape from England", Gunther Plüschow
ISBN 1-904466-21-4
In either World War, only one German escaped from mainland Britain: Gunther Plüschow. "Escape From England" tells his story.
This book also gives a unique account of the siege of Tsingtao in 1914 and Plüschow's amazing escape from China across the Pacific to America and then to Europe.

"The Escaping Club", A.J. Evans
ISBN 1-904466-27-3
Describing Evans' escape from Fort 9 (the Great War equivalent of Colditz), this is undoubtably one of the greatest escape books of all time.

"Across Africa", V.L. Cameron
ISBN 1-904466-26-5
The first European to cross Central Africa from East to West. V.L. Cameron's "Across Africa" is essential reading for anyone interested in the exploration of the then Dark Continent.

"Let's Go Climbing!", Colin Kirkus
ISBN 1-904466-17-6
"Let's Go Climbing!" was written by legendary climber Colin Kirkus as an introduction to the sport of mountaineering. One of the most engaging books ever written, it was read and revered by both Joe Brown and Don Whillans. In the world of British climbing, there is probably no greater compliment.

"My Climbs in the Alps and Caucasus", A.F. Mummery,
ISBN 1-904466-09-5
Fred Mummery's rousing and humorous account of his European climbing career is a mountaineering classic. Years ahead of his time, Mummery and his companions were the first to climb without guides: they laid the future for modern mountaineering as we know it today.

"From the Himalaya to Skye", Norman Collie
ISBN 1-904466-08-7
This is Norman Collie's own account of Mummery's last expedition – the 1895 attempt on Nanga Parbat. The book also contains Collie's accounts of his climbs on Skye, the Canadian Rockies, Wasdale and on Tower Ridge.

"Norway: the Northern Playground", Cecil Slingsby,
ISBN 1-904466-07-9
The story of the first ascents of many of Norway's most dramatic peaks, Slingsby's book is still a very relevant guidebook to many Norwegian mountain areas today.

"Travels Amongst the Great Andes of the Equator", Edward Whymper.
ISBN 1-904466-24-9
This is Edward Whymper's successful expedition to the Ecuadorian Andes, including the active volcano Cotopaxi. It is a worthy successor to his classic book "Scrambles Amongst the Alps".

Appendix 5

Pictures from "The Borderers"

Editor's note:

"The Borderers" is a small group of enthusiasts, from all over Britain (as well as some members who travel across from the Netherlands) who come together in order to pursue and research the way of life of the Border Reivers and is carried out through a programme of "Living History".

I am grateful to them for providing both the cover pictures and for the pictures included in this Appendix.

The group is based at Old Buittle Tower in Dumfries and Galloway Region in the South West of Scotland, not too far from the old West March mentioned in Carey's memoirs. The Tower is home to Jeffrey and Janet Burn who provide the facilities used by the society, which include horses, stables, a forge, a dyeing facility and a recreated Period Kitchen and Medieval Hall.

The work of the Society can be seen by the public at weekend shows. The Easter and August Bank Holidays events are open to the general public. More specialized weekends are held approximately every six weeks throughout the year, starting with our Christmas Fayre held in early December. Admission to these events is by pre-booked ticket.

More details are available at the Borderers website http://www.theborderers.info/index.html

The pictures below should give another insight into the life and times of Robert Carey.

High Table

Ray Schofield

Keith Piggott

Sean Barbour

Foot Louns

About Ripping Yarns.com

There are a lot of classic adventure books which are undeservedly now out of print and unavailable to the general public. In today's mass-market publishing world they would be likely to remain that way.

Ripping Yarns.com was started in 2002 to publish out-of-print adventure books on the Internet in e-book form. Since then, we have grown and are now producing classic adventure books in conventional paperback and hardback form.

We hope to ensure that these classic tales are once again available and not forgotten.

If you enjoyed this book, please visit our website for more rip-roaring adventure titles.

www.RippingYarns.com